CURTAIN SPEECH

the author as Marie Antoinette, 2012

PHOTO BY MARK ROCKWOOD

CURTAIN
SPEECH

an actor's poems about the theatre

Ellen Adair

PEN & ANVIL

ISBN 978-0-9821625-6-9 (paperback)

Printed in the United States of America.

An earlier version of this collection was circulated privately from 2015. This trade edition contains additional poems and an updated introduction and notes.

The author wishes to acknowledge the prior appearance of the poems "Life's a Colander" and "Unrequited" in *Clarion*, of "Pegeen" in *Cypher*, of "Eating Verse" in *Oddball*, and of "Thomasina's Poem to Be Lost", "The One-Letter O-Word", "Theatrechurch" and "Entropy and Conservation" in *The Charles River Journal*.

A note on the page layout: Where a stanza break coincides with a page break, the leading page is marked with an asterisk beside the page number.

Cover design and text layout by Zachary Bos.

Pen & Anvil Press   *www.penandanvil.com*

CONTENTS

Part III : RAINA

Part IV : MARY

Part V : SHAKESPEARE

Part VI : ACTORS

Illustrations, drawn by the author: 22 : Pegeen, in *Playboy of the Western World.* 58 : Septimus and Plautus; drawn onstage during a performance of *Arcadia.* 68 : Raina's souvenir photograph for Captain Bluntschli, torn during onstage action. 78 : Mary Shelley at sixteen, and her shadow. 90 : Bust of Shakespeare owned by the author, inherited from her father. 114 : Mary and Charlie in *Mary's Wedding.* 128 : The spirit in the theatrechurch.

FOREWORD

A FEW YEARS AGO I received an e-mail from a young actor. Nothing unusual in that, as for thirty-five years I have run professional theatres and communications from actors requesting, pleading or sometimes demanding consideration for a role are as ubiquitous as they are easily ignored. E-mails, in fact, are easier to ignore than actual letters. There is something about hitting "delete" that feels less callous than discarding a picture, resume and the sometimes heartfelt, more often formulaic and not infrequently borderline-illiterate letter. But this letter was different.

I had written a play about Byron, Shelley, Mary Wollstonecraft Godwin *et al*, and the (undoubtedly well known to any reader of poetry) famous summer of 1816 at the Villa Diodati near Geneva, and the ghost story competition that became the genesis of Mary Shelley's *Frankenstein*. It had been announced for the season at the Pioneer Theatre Company in Salt Lake City and, as is required by Actors' Equity Association, a breakdown describing the available roles in the play was posted in the Equity offices in New York preceding open auditions for the theatre's season.

The letter described the actor's astonishment at seeing the notice on the Equity callboard and learning of a play focusing on those characters and events. It went on to announce the actor's passion for the Romantic poets, Shelley in particular. I believe she wrote something to the effect, "Having spent my entire education split between the study of the Romantic poets and the practice of theatre, I have sometimes idly commented I am fit for nothing now but to play Mary Shelley."

At that point in time, the play, *The Yellow Leaf* had accumulated several staged readings but not yet a full production. Several sets of actors had read the play from music stands to small invited audiences so that I could have the opportunity of hearing the play out loud and producers could consider it for production. In the brief rehearsals for those projects I was not overly surprised at the unfamiliarity of many of the actors with the specific events and tangled relationships of "the year without a summer" at the Villa Diodati, but in several instances I was utterly astonished at the blank stares of incomprehension at the names Byron, Shelley, Mary Godwin. (You know, they don't teach poetry in most high schools anymore, nor in the puffed-up trade schools that many universities pass off as "Actor Training Programs"—but don't get me started.) But, they were actors after all (and sometimes good ones) so I made allowances and when I mentioned Ken Russell's terrible film on the subject, *Gothic*, I several times sparked a glimmer of recognition, not infrequently followed by: "You mean that actually happened? Cool!"

So, when I received Ms. Adair's letter—yes, obviously, she was the young actor or why would you be reading this at all—I was intrigued by the fact that here was an actor who not only knew the subject I was writing about in some depth, but, yes, even more flattering, was excited by it. So, I wrote her back, noting that I would not be present at the Equity open call, therefore there was not much point for her in attending and that specific auditions for the play would be held in New York in November and if she would send me a picture and resume I would try to remember to have the casting director call her in to audition at the appropriate time. At the end of my response, I added a postscript something to the effect: "You'll really impress me if you can tell me to what the title, *The Yellow Leaf* refers?" I didn't really expect a response to my flippant and slightly condescending question other than the requested picture and resume. But I patted myself on the back for being nice and not having callously punched "delete."

So, when she responded immediately, nailing the reference to Byron's last poem, "On This Day I Complete My Thirty-Sixth Year," with the added bonus that Byron's image of faded vitality was in fact lifted by the poet from Act V of *Macbeth*, I admit, I was kind of impressed.

A few months later she auditioned for the world premiere production of *The Yellow Leaf*. The director, Geoffrey Sherman, chose to cast her with my happy agreement. The play rehearsed. It opened. It closed. We called it a success. We became friends. She asked to read some of my other plays and at some point she told me she was also a writer, a poet mostly, but with a novel underway as well, and I said, "Well, show me some of your stuff if you want to." She did.

And then I was really impressed. And remain so to this day. This is a writer. Not an actor who writes to fill the time between jobs or the boring off-stage gaps in technical rehearsals or to create material for embarrassingly personal performance art. This is a real writer.

Not only is Ms. Adair a young actor of intelligence, talent and sensitivity with a joyous and collaborative spirit, but she has—as the reader will soon discover—a remarkable gift for language, an extraordinary ability for sometimes ear startling imagery and the insight and intelligence to put those gifts to use in the service of complex and interesting ideas.

The poems in *Curtain Speech* are ostensibly about the theatre, acting, the actor's process, and some of the authors and characters Ms. Adair has played in her young career. But all these poems live far below the surface of their subject matter and are really all about "being" and "seeming;" about the actor that lives in all of us, about the very nature of story-telling, language and narrative.

It doesn't hurt to know something about theatre process, the plays and the playwrights she references in *Curtain Speech*, but it certainly isn't a necessity. Like all good writing, ultimately Ellen Adair writes about what it means to be human.

Charles Morey
playwright and director
New York City

PREFACE

FOR THOSE SEEKING AN INTRODUCTION:

I am a professional actor. These are my poems about different characters, acting, and a life in the theatre.

For those (aggrieved, possibly) seeking a more complex explanation for what they will find here:

As is so often the case, the chain of blame leads back to my parents, who brought me, at age seven, to see the film version of Kenneth Branagh's *Henry V*. I loved it so much that I made them take me back four more times, so clearly something in my nature, as well as nurture, is culpable. I was in my first Shakespeare play at age twelve (in the age- and gender-appropriate role of Julius Caesar) which means I have been doing Shakespeare for well over half my life.

While shooting a commercial a few summers ago, a fellow-actor asked me, in a conversation about writing, who my greatest influence was. Strangely enough, I had never been asked this question directly, so it was in the very moment that I discovered the answer. I told him that though probably everyone would say the same thing, it was Shakespeare. My kind conversant replied that he did not think it a typical answer at all. Whatever the case, this fact is for my part is indisputable.

However, the influence on my writing is not as a reader but as a performer of Shakespeare's text, and the ramifications of this distinction are manifold. The first is that Shakespearean language is actually alive in the mouths of actors speaking his words around the globe. It happens in nearly every production, as far as I've witnessed: Shakespearean words or phrasing will get picked up by the cast, perhaps as a joke at first, but increasingly unconsciously, as any words do—think, for example, of the way a culture absorbs slang. My half-lifetime of Shakespearean vernacular has a clear result. For example, because I played Costard in *Love's Labour's Lost* at the age of fourteen, the word 'remuneration' is as likely to occur to me for use in a conversation as would the word 'payment.' I have become a person who uses a thesaurus chiefly to find a less-complicated synonym. I have a clear memory of turning to my best friend in college, and asking her: "What would be a less-complicated word for 'besmirch'? 'Sully'?" I'm a ridiculous construction, I know. I don't aim to be archaic; that's just the way language is in my head. Because classical actors use those words night after night, year after year, they are not anachronisms; they are ours.

I have noticed that Shakespeare's iambs too have worked their way into my unconscious. I am sometimes regimented enough to write purposefully in meter—in the following pages, poems whose lines are first letter capitalizatized are intentionally metrical—but even when the number of feet per line varies, I've found iambic rhythms frequently work their way in. All of this, I suppose, is the influence of a profession in which poetry is meant to be heard, not read.

I own the influence is not wholly an unconscious one, and perhaps its most important aspect is my conscious and professed love of the *muscularity* of Shakespearean language. I am unabashedly envious of early modern English's allowance to bend grammar to fit meaning. I know our language is not at present the flexible thing it once was, but all of these years of speaking Shakespeare have made me feel that I ought to be able to make words into different parts of speech, or to jam words together to make new ones. (Did you know 'bedroom' is a Shakespearean kenning?) I like language that's *doing* something, and believe the action of the language adds timbre and color to its mere meaning. Though many a high school freshman may beg to differ with me, Shakespeare's text is not convoluted as a rule; sometimes it's very straightforward, and that's part of the information. If a line is a little hard to understand, it's probably telling you something about the character's state of mind.

In summation:

My appreciation of what is good in writing and what is good in acting has an emblem in the form of a line from Hamlet's advice to the players—

Suit the action to the word, the word to the action.

If I were in a profession where a huge and hard-to-cover tattoo weren't a professional liability, I would have that line tattooed hugely on me. As all actors know, action is life's muscle: you ought to be trying to *do* something, or to *get* something. I have found I like my own writing to be trying to do something, too; I want to suit the action of the language to the event it describes. I may fail but in my writing as in my acting, I consider it nobler to fail at doing than to have never ventured the effort.

Ellen Adair
New York City

TIMELINE

of the author's performances

1998

» *A Midsummer Night's Dream*, Indiana Shakespeare Co., Bloomington IN

2004

» *Pygmalion*, Longwood Players, Boston MA (Addison Award for Best Actress)

2005

» *A Midsummer Night's Dream*, ShakespeareNow, Boston MA
» *Romeo and Juliet*, ShakespeareNow
» *Macbeth*, ShakespeareNow
» *Arcadia*, Publick Theatre, Boston MA (IRNE nomination for Best Actress; Elliot Norton Award for Best Production)
» *Comedy of Errors*, Publick Theatre
» *John James Audubon: Drawn from Nature*, PBS/Florentine Films
» *A Doll's House*, Small World Big Sky Productions, Boston MA (Addison Award for Best Ensemble)
» *Carol Mulroney*, Huntington Theatre Co., Boston MA
» *Brotherhood*, Showtime
» *My Sister, the Psychopath*, short film

2006

» *Five by Tenn*, SpeakEasy Stage Co., Boston MA (Elliot Norton Award for Best Production)
» *Macbeth*, New Repertory Theater On Tour, Boston MA
» *All's Well That Ends Well*, Actors' Shakespeare Project, Boston MA
» *The Beard of Avon*, Publick Theatre, Boston MA
» *By the Bog of Cats*, Devanaughn Theater, Boston MA
» *The Diary of Anne Frank*, New Repertory Theater on Tour
» *Rabbit Hole*, Huntington Theatre Co., Boston MA

2007

» *Romeo & Juliet's Ball* (gala), Actors' Shakespeare Project, Boston MA
» *More Than What*, Centastage, Boston MA (world premiere)
» *Louis Brandeis: The People's Attorney*, PBS/Charles Stuart Productions
» *Arms and the Man*, Lyric Stage Co., Boston MA
» *Louisa May Alcott: The Woman Behind* Little Women, PBS/Nancy Porter Productions
» *A Christmas Carol*, American Shakespeare Center, Staunton VA

2007-8

» national tour with American Shakespeare Center: *The Taming of the Shrew; The Merchant of Venice; Henry V*

2008

» *Henry IV, Part One*, Folger Theater, Washington DC

2009

» *The Yellow Leaf*, Pioneer Theater Co., Salt Lake City UT (world premiere)
» *'Tis Pity She's a Whore*, Baltimore Centerstage, Baltimore MD
» *God in America*, PBS
» *As the World Turns*, CBS
» *Fourplay*, Secret Room Theater, Philadelphia Fringe Festival, Philadelphia PA
» *The Playboy of the Western World*, Pearl Theatre Co., NYC
» *A Family Joint*, short film

2010

» *Romeo and Hamlet*, GayfestNYC, NYC (US premiere)
» *As the World Turns*, CBS
» *Major Barbara* (Reading), Project Shaw, Gingold Theatrical Group, NYC
» *The Playboy of the Western World*, Pennsylvania Shakespeare Festival, Center Valley PA
» *All's Well That Ends Well*, Shakespeare Theatre of New Jersey, Madison NJ

2011

» *What the Public Wants*, Mint Theatre, NYC
» *Light Falling* (gala event), Mint Theatre, NYC
» *Mary's Wedding*, Kitchen Theatre, Ithaca NY
» *Cymbeline*, Barrow St. Theatre/Theatre for a New Audience/Fiasco Theater, NYC (Off-Broadway Alliance Award for Best Revival)

2012

» *Red Light Winter*, Kitchen Theatre, Ithaca NY (BroadwayWorld nomination for Best Actress)
» *Christian et Christine*, short film
» *Marie Antoinette: The Color of Flesh*, Portland Stage Co., Portland ME
» *The Straw* (reading), Peccadillo Theater Co., NYC
» *Sleep No More* (special events), Punchdrunk, NYC
» *Victor Frange Presents GAS*, Incubator Arts, NYC (world premiere)

2013

» *Ryan Landry's "M,"* Huntington Theater Co., Boston MA (world premiere)
» *The Two Gentlemen of Verona*, Commonwealth Shakespeare Co., Boston MA
» *The Mousetrap*, Repertory Theatre of St. Louis, St. Louis MO
» *The Unwanted*, feature film

2014

- *Nurse Jackie,* Showtime
- *As You Like It,* Happy Few Theatre Co., NYC (NY Innovative Theatre Award nominations, Outstanding Ensemble Performance and Outstanding Revival)
- *Private Lives,* Shakespeare Theatre Co., Washington DC
- *Veep,* HBO
- *Codes of Conduct,* (pilot) HBO
- *Chitty Chitty Bailey Chang,* web series

2015

- *The Slap,* NBC
- *No Margrettes,* short film
- *Through the Night,* short film
- *The Importance of Being Earnest,* Titan Theatre Co., NYC
- *The Family,* ABC

2016

- *The Blacklist,* NBC
- *the goodbye room,* Happy Few Theatre Company, NYC (world premiere)
- *I Love You But I Lied,* LMN
- *Season of Passage,* short film
- *Detroit, I Love You* (pilot)
- *Rainbow City,* short film

2017

- *Billions,* Showtime
- *Constellations,* St. Louis Repertory Theatre, St. Louis MO
- *The Suitcase Under the Bed,* Mint Theatre Company, NYC
- *Shades of Blue,* NBC

2018

- *Homeland,* Showtime
- *The Sinner,* USA
- *Compliance,* FX (pilot)
- *Chicago Fire,* NBC
- *Sins of the Son,* short film
- *Roommating,* web series
- *Fireside,* short film
- *Love and Communication,* feature film
- *Red Dead Redemption 2,* videogame

for all the actors
with whom I've worked

but especially
for Eric

who makes
both life & art
so good

CURTAIN SPEECH

Actor

When the hand becomes transparent,
the self translucent, the background apparent
through the center, it becomes necessary to define a doll
for your own self, out of paper.

This is mine. The base:

these are the rioting bones of my feet.

This is the forbidden hub of the ribspokes,
excessive as a star.

This is my skin, punctuated
with the sun's declarative sentences.

This bare body, as humble and arrogant
as all who feel they are the last of a dying race.

These costumes:

boy, woman,
brilliant child,
subtraction

of the centuries.

Dress me up.

I.
CHARACTERS

DEIRDRE: *It should be a sweet thing to have what is best
and richest, if it's for a short space only.*

– John Millington Synge, *Deirdre of the Sorrows*

Flesh and Blood

A character is like a child
in her constant need for love,
in the way she will not tire
of drinking up your love,
like adults, who sicken.

A character is like a parent
in her patience,
in the way she scoops you up,
and that whole life she lived
before you came.

To Eliza (Present)

O child of mine sexlessly conceived
by the bright firewater of God shot down
into my spine, into the original pen
that double-deity creates, splits the second's skull
to bring the unchild full-armoured from the mind,
o child of a dead man whose adult gestation
was in my hairwide womb: you are more myself

than I am. Are you therefore
more me than yourself, or do we gemini ourselves
in skin like a room made from one wall, both
mortared in the caulking of the brick,
glove each other in the hallways
of the smallest divisible particle?
I would ask you, which of us is me,
the changed or the original; but that is your question
too. I have stolen it and am calling it my own.

You seem more me because you're wrought
only from the ore of self most pure,
with none of the indigestible assumptions
that compose reality. I am not this I.
Everything else could be called me as easily.
But I could divide myself along your lines,
say that where you end
the probability of me starts dropping
towards the eternal almost-zero.

But in the sole illumination
of the streetlamp banded through the blinds,
Eliza in the mirror says:
You know very well all the time
that you are nothing but illusion.
My body is the home you seek,

the life that time has stripped from you.
I carry you seedsized somewhere
in the folds of my red depths.
I am your immaculate mother.

To Eliza (Departed)

Afterwards, my body collapsed
as if the tentpoles had been taken out,

as if my shoulder-coat had bowed
off the swinging hanger.

You have left me like an orphan child
with the photograph of you

recopied in my eyes and nose, the appearance
that others will not recognize is yours.

Sonnet for Geoffrey

The centre contracts and the limbs flop loose,
like a fist that holds two ropes together.
Arms out like parentheses,
swinging like bird shoulderfeathers.
Especially under the knees
the shins flail above the shuffling heels.
Especially above the knees
the body draws into its x.
But look down at the hands: damned
woman's hands that cannot persuade
me to say, —These are Geoffrey's hands,
not Ludibundus's, Cleopatra's, Kate's.
Damned woman's face, only disappearance
of all mirrors could make me think it is a boy's.

Geoffrey's Riposte

Nay. Thou wrongst me.
Leave this ado of gender
of which I tire.
For I am most like thee

of any, ever,
being the first actor
or act-ress you have played:
so I am also made

out of the zero and the egg,
the everything and nothing.

Hanging Out

When you and I slounge about
in the hot-slick days
and the nights starred
with mosquitoes, our mouths
dribble with curses.

Later, *Fuck* catapults
from my lip. Potty mouth,
chides my friend, used to me
blasting and poohing
like a moderately scandalous
nineteenth-century girl.

Hanging out with Geoffrey
makes me swear, I explained.
He swears as innocently and as often
as a lamb drops poop.
He's your character,
my friend interjects.

No: I am his.

Actor/Actress

A great delight of my daily life
is riding on the post-show subway
with my boyplayer's woman's makeup
still Kabuki-masked upon my face.

Paperpowder white, with two
red suns upon my cheeks,
and three dots of deathred
bowing up my lips,

I have seen the little unpainted children
from the corner of my contoured eye
with the dots of their finger-points
and their mouths bowed open.

Tonight, standing on the platform
as the incoming train blurred by,
I saw, clear as an angel,
a transvestite, flying, leaning

against the wings of the train doors.
We stared at each other for the eternity
of a second. We were both confused,
both recognised ourselves inside the other.

Lady Lettice's Poem

I hear you dined with Leicester yestereve.
He flinches still beneath your regal gaze,
We both still flinch and scurry like the mice
Who conspired against the whisker-ruffèd cat.

The night you turned me out, behowling 'She-Wolf'
At me, and spurred on your pack of fops,
The blackness seemed to swarm in at my eyes,
The roadsides seemed to streak out from the palace.

The lights like music blared inside the court,
The only sound abroad in the whole world
Was the running of my shoes, the shame
Wrung out of my lashes. But I tire

Of running, Majesty, Virgin Queen,
Virgin to the inch of your white paint.
I tire of paying obeisance
To the eternal spectre of your glare,

To your Martyrdom to Everything.
Do not blame me alone for marrying
When you never would have married him,
Would have refused to stoop and bear his child.

To Nora

The tunnel of the evening.
Sometimes so hard to keep
the face arranged. Every night
I think, Teach me who I am.

You are that porcelain
I see in the nighted windowpane,
ossified below the surface
and steel sheathed in the eyes.

Armour of the corset. We will
get through together.

My Mr. Paradise

O fatherpoet, who has stayed at sight's
Periphery with a face as tragic
As a bird, forgive my inattention,
And do not make me old before my time.

O loosen me of coldness in this world
Where to be trodden is the best accessory.
I am tired of this age where youth
Fashions cynicism in its eyes,

Until I wish that I could compensate
By keeping green the stalks that have been bent.
Already I'm aware of those halftruths
Endurance sells us in exchange for days,
Love and art's expectations crashing:

That knowledge is fair payment for potential
That we lose in getting it; that someday
The world will grow more ceremonious,
And all lost beauty I have fought to save
Will be picked up by one or two and turned
In their fingers like an ancient coin.

Unrequited

I will tell you. The person I love
will only meet me at certain hours
when there are others present.
She set out the date when our
affair will end: then she will not come back.
Sometimes she doesn't show up anyway,
maybe because I've taken her for granted,
and my lone hands are left to play
like puppets with each other.

She is hard-won, her rabbit eyes watching
and her heart at a violet-high frequency.
After weeks of squatting still and collecting
her actions and gestures, collecting my love,
then she'll inch out of the ring of the leaves.

But once she loves me, it is more God
than anything else found below heaven's eaves.

I am afraid to explain precisely
how much of a visiting spirit she is.
You'll think I'm mad or pretentious
when I say she comes down like a goddess.

The hard part is we've both had many lovers.
And then she's always the one to leave, apologetically
taking her words and her clothes, shrugging,
smiling like It's Not You, It's Me.

And me pleading, No don't leave
me with this sole self, the husk of us.

To someone else it must seem as unrequited
as both Echo and Narcissus for Narcissus.

To an outsider, my love must seem the same
as all those painful girlish years I spent,
umbrella-awkward, body bent,
kissing doorframes.

To Caroline

i.

We fit not like the proverbial
glove to the hand, but like two
too-small white handgloves
handless, nestled empty
inside each other.

ii.

Unlike any other, you have cracked
emotion's egg over all my body,
its raw fluid gumming up my limbs.
Suddenly, the chessboard
of the rehearsal room askew.

Because the director said, —You cannot
go to him, you cannot be so obvious;
and our overlaid hearts were breached,
no single finger capable of stopping up the dam.
You burned at me until I thought our body would be ash.

I must remember you live
in an unostentatious country,
where the poet must not
sing his own songs, or he will grow
appendages of arrogance.

iii.

But in the end, one of us
is only wearing the other
like a thin holed slip, mutually
eyewettened, clinging; and I
am not sure I am not worn.

Caroline: The Unspoken

i.

Voice
   birdthroatcaught
In a place where talk
pins the tragedy back,
I am silent.

I do not offer gossip
against death and wetness,
the lining of the days.

The houses are only haystack humps
around an unblaze like a needle.
Each family huddled round
remembrance of the turf.

Who will take the quiet I have kept
and mould it to a dove
like the branchbeaked one
that came after the flood?

ii.

I am

that space

you see there.

That. White

not even like
snow but that sterilised
surgical white, that death-room
white like the sheet
pulled over my mother's body and
eventually
her head.

I
used
to be communionwhite
but the things that touched

smeared like sodstuck
boots, tramping
through

and the eye on the end
like a gun.

Mother could do no laundry
in the ground, so I took out
all my insides,
brought them to the back
of the house, and elbowhigh
scrubbed them clean.
And hung them.

Inside was so

white again,
I did not put them back.

iii.

Only the air
holds me, and look
how it keeps receding
as I walk.

All the water
in my father's
land keeps leaping up.
That's why it's always hanging

in the air.
Clinging to the skin.
My body is transgression
on the universe.

I am a high, unnecessary
thing, like a plastic bag
streaming accidental
on the fingers of a tree.

iv. *Other*

The time has come
for you to give up
what you've already lost.

The time has come
for your wraith to stop
appearing heartless

on every greenspined lane,
behind me in the mirrorpane,
with black-air hands

moving objects in my room.
You'll make ghosts
of both of us.

    iv. *Husband*

The word
mocks. Until you give
a straw out of that bundle,

I
must not show my enormity
of care.

The discrepancy
would break
my head off like a doll's,

would dissipate
my antiquated shade,
with its scars at last

surfaced as it roams
the battlefield that's every inch
of this island's dirt.

    vi.

But of course no dissipation comes.
We all persist long after
in unfit situations.

We have been bred
this way,
to be

like the land
no one in their right mind
would farm.

   viii.

I am the corner
tucked behind the cupboard.
I am the Room you never
sit in, hoping to keep it clean,

but mostly keeping it vacant.
I know I am the periphery, but still I feel
like everyone falls away from me
like dead petals from the stalk.

Perhaps I am an altered photograph.
I have been cut
out and glued into another
picture, with my outline visible.

Or else I was glued into
nothing afterwards,
the white background now
extending endlessly

Dialogue of the Double Self

Actor.　　　　I wish I could become encased in you
　　　　like veins inside a leaf, and not return.

Character.　　You have it backwards.
　　　　I am sealed inside
　　　　the container of your body.
　　　　I was born blind
　　　　as the pen and page.
　　　　Try to see as me without
　　　　opening your eyes. You will see
　　　　I have none of my own.

Actor.　　　　I see now it is my duty
　　　　to carry you around to see
　　　　the world that is your own.
　　　　I am the outermost layer, skinthin,
　　　　the film on the sight that is yours,
　　　　my bare molecular layer hardly holds you in.
　　　　I am a casing, a costume of you,
　　　　your fission sends out my limbs:
　　　　you are all the angel
　　　　and I am all the dust upon her hands.

The Director: To Galatea

Untime ages I waited in the pre-difference of dark and light;
before the beams that you reflect were focused,
I figured the space for you; before you existed,
I had a sculpture made of air for you to fit in.

Like God, who set the mobile of the planets
and the sun for them, who made the black fabric between
out of His soul, I have dispersed myself.
I am partly in every atom, and wholly in none.

This is why God says, Think of me above,
and drifted on the expansion impulse.
Think of where it is only me, stranded in blank,
divided by galaxies of smiles.

Like Michelangelo, I took the rock and cut away
all the parts that were not you, and so cut away myself.
It is your breath that I taught you to take
out of the air-space I made you.

O stone turned autonomous, you are no consolation.
How you would laugh to learn how unGodlike I am,
how you infected me with the common cold
of all sweet sadnesses, unrequited love.

World Premiere

i. *Metaphors of First*

1.
Like stout Cortez
I gaze upon the script's horizon line—
the native author foraged here before me,
the director made a survey of the coast.

But still the wild wavecaps
daze me. Still my body
carves an unknown shape
above the untouched beach.

2.
I am the first to walk into this temple.
Not that the paving stones leap up
from non-existence where my toe touches down,
or the pillars collapse upwards out of air—
this building was constructed by a master architect,
so that such a one as I
might enter it.

But I am accustomed
to following a floor worn smooth
by centuries of feet, to lead me
where I lay down my last lit leastlight candle
at an altar that is a prairie made of flame.

Yet still it smells of stone here,
like a cave. My gradual feet
shuffle on the pearly flagstone
to place a solitary incense stick
into the gleaming golden bowl.

Its smoke winds up to where the sculpture's face
is still draped inside the darkness.

ii. *Relationships*

1.
The first few days
we both walk

with lambwobbly
coltjointed legs,

and I feel as eggfresh
as you, not sure how to hold

the softnecked head
of anything so modern.

2.
You accepted me because I was your first.
A young girl shown affection
cannot tell if it is clumsy, undeserving.

You came so faithfully
it shamed me. Every day
you came with fingers like Persephone

before she was ever swooped into the dark.
I whispered, 'I love you'
in the pitch behind the curtain

and you came, each time,
your eyes flung open, your skull
quivering with light.

I did
love you, but I shuddered
at your innocence, that you did not

know I'd loved many
before you, and many
more than you.

    iii. *Evolution*

1.
Because you can never be worthy
of being First,
there is no ample preparation.

The First is a creature
that in the night's middle
spontaneously evolves a skeleton
out of the bare air's natural selection.

The First is God with a cape of stars.
The First is a purple explosion,
lizards vaulting out of the sea.
How can one descended from an endless line
of life, be First in anything?

2.
I fumbled for you
like a person in an unlit bedroom
fumbles for glasses on the nightstand.

Like the foot looks for the next step
and finds air.

Like a surgical procedure with no light.

But I fell asleep with these glasses on.
One who runs out of stairs

arrives in Heaven. And when
I operate from within my body,
no light slices up the warmsweet dark.

Week Four Doldrums

All the more therefore I bend
my five human powers in your service,
and dedicate my life down to its end
in exchange for your five eternities.

When honesty tatters into difficulty,
all the more I keep my office holy.
I am just the chrome on the machine:
you are its goldrippling gasoline.

That is why I know delight will spring
up every night at my offering,
as tirelessly as the globerock's endless spinning
brings about another winter's ending.

Pegeen

Half a lifetime before my mouth
housed your words, I loved you.

Half a year before my body
boarded your bright spirit, I was pinning
tears up in my backstage separation,
stuck just bringing in the petticoat
on his famous line about the shifts,
feeling I'd be as grateful for your soul
as a man with miles of desert on his knees
would be for dew from angels' wings.

I felt that from the first, for this
you'd love me like no other ever had.

And I gave you almost every jewel
and flower, plume, star or sun I owned,
bartered more of my self daily
for your greater honesty,
gratefully praised God as I ate
your Queenfeet and sidethumb
and you lapped and lapped
the white lake of my mind.

I threw my heart down for your carpet.
I tossed down little fragments
chipped from my marbled soul.
I tore up and down my throat for you.
I bruised every room inside my ribs.
I lashed my body to you
until our tears became identical,
and came to hate my self to that vomit pitch,

to that same horror at the rope and bellows,
til I was never sure if your full fury
lashed me because I gave too little, or too much.

To Emily

You only you know me.
I only I (of those alive)
know you. I am infinitely
(like a mirror to a mirror)
astounded that when I lay
my head to your sternum,
or we yoke our arms over
one another's shoulders,

the action is invisible.

For Mary (Present)

Our inked hearts laid to paper
would reveal indistinguishable prints:
the whorls and arches ridging the same way.

All characters before
have had their bodies tailored
from my truth reorganised,

but our hearts' targets are identical,
that same proud-lipped strungbow jaw,
that sweet gaze feather-fringed:

my metaphor of him becomes his function actual,
and on the pin of this central truth,
your skin slips on me without alteration.

For Mary (Departed)

You and I have been so close
you sometimes were invisible,

and I wonder, now that you too are gone
into the rain-specked grass,

if I took you for granted
the way we take ourselves

for granted, that first assumption
each day the eyelids keep

opening after sleep.
I wonder, did I fail to love you enough,

mostly loving him you loved,
or was this finally the service

all characters deserve?
Maybe the way I miss

you is the same way I will miss
my body the day after I've mis-

placed it, that joy of joint and muscle,
of radiance and sprout.

After the Death

Like opening the closet
to all the flat unbodied shirts,
finding a scrap of handwriting (here,

the hand was) finding a frameless
photograph floating in a drawer,
finding a ring, a hairbrush, soap,

my fingers pull your fingers out
like a possession unexpected
in the bathroom cabinet.

I was fine until I stooped to pick a flower
and saw it with your eye
and used your hand.

You were my inside bodified
more justly than myself.
Though you held me in your arms

when you spun your final breath,
your funeral is casketless,
like a soldier's who disappeared

in an unknown land,
simply exchanged
life for air.

II.
THOMASINA

THOMASINA: *Oh, Septimus! — can you bear it? ...How can we sleep for grief?*

SEPTIMUS: *By counting our stock... We shed as we pick up, like travellers who must carry everything in their arms, and what we let fall will be picked up by those behind. The procession is very long and life is very short. We die on the march. But there is nothing outside the march so nothing can be lost to it.*

– Tom Stoppard, *Arcadia*

Thomasina's First Two Gifts

i. *A Vision on my Eyelid*

There is a girl whose spirit blows
off the ends of her curled hair
and the lines of her white skirts.
She is standing in the garden,
turning to the mansion,
she is burning at the edges.

ii. *A Song*

And then my tears leapt only because
My skin is as thin as a paper,
And the blue and the gold of the world rushes through
The holes on my limbs like stars.

The atoms that travel are brimming with love
And transfer their charge to my breastbone,
Love of a girl from two centuries past,
With a birthplace over the ocean,

And currently breathing, and born in my lungs,
Sharpened on space and softened on art,
On the blue and the gold of the world rushing through
My skin's arrangement of stars.

To Thomasina

All my self-world ills
Are remedied by love
Of a thirteen-year-old girl.

The sparklers of your fingers
And the torchstick of your spine
Have lifted me in ecstasy:
O take me in your arms again.

We both joyed when the nineteenth-century clouds
Were brimming with the fierce sublime, the grey
In them as thick as wine and drinkable;
The raindrops hung off of the stage like lace,
The breaking sun made curtains of their streaks:

O take me in your elevated brain, o take
Me in the squaring of your heart, that asks o take
Me in your lifted arms, and put these arms inside
Your arms that ask me put me in your waltzing arms,
Sustain my burning youth inside the corners of
Your unplumbed eyes, spin me in infinity.

Thomasina's Poem for Septimus

My dearest Septimus—

Nothing rhymes with your name,
and I do not mean the word
'nothing' rhymes, only the unword
that does not exist.

This being the pre-existing
situation, I suppose it is convenient
that I am adequate at mathematics;
for even if your name were Sam,
I have not much skill at rhymes,
nor could you be won by them;
so I will write you poems
without words, give you
the Metaphor of Everything.

Thomasina's Poem to Be Lost to the Sands of Time

I have tried this hour to express how absolutely tedious
everyone is being, chasing that poet around
and a new set chasing the chasers,

but I have been stopped from mocking them
by my lack of a rhyming jibe.
Pooh.

Why do poems need rhymes at all?
I prophesy that one day they will explode
like everything else.

To Thomasina, Dying

Child, how can I hold you in my lap?
How can I make separate hands for you, for me
to clutch? What will I do when your skin slips off
(you have made my skin correctly fit

finally), when calm and pink you're laid
inside the coffin of the turned-off light?
What black Atlantic will my sight become
once the burnmark of your eyes is gone?

Your eyes' shade is mine, but your pupil's core
tightens, loosens so much swifter
than my own. Do not leave.
For I will have to live after your death.

To Thomasina, One Year Later

I watched the branchtips play the sky
like a piano, and remembered watching
the identical configuration of Sidley Park.
The Park has since picked up
and moved elsewhere on the earth,

but I remember feeling your eyes
dilate at the sight, and felt you
hover now, haunting the place you lived,
trying to pat my wettened cheek.
You were the first to show how my eyes

could be replaced by yours.
Out of my humanity's wide hoop, your sphere
approximated me better than my own.
Though my current characters always rebel
when I say so, and for days will not speak to me,

I loved you most.
When I sensed you there,
my body swarmed with stars,
my eyeholes contracted and I wept:
we have both turned into nothing.

To Thomasina, Six Years Later

Once in the intermission bathroom stall,
my hemmedup tears let fall.

I am ridiculous, like a onetrick
weeping pony. I thought six

years ample time to see you, finally,
in someone else's body.

But I cried because (in your words)
time cannot be unstirred,

because (as they say) you can't go home;
because that home that I've been cast from,

a stately place with all the ceremony
and passion of a summered tree,

is not a home I've ever known,
is not a home that might be found,

and all this is blindly stitching
a quilt from imitation silk.

Candle for Thomasina, or, Theatrechurch's Failing

If I thought that I could see you when I die,
that in heaven all my characters would come
clustering like cherubs, and you in pink with your sparking
    fingers
would come running down the lawn and hit into my body
like a tank of water released from its container,

if there were any philosophy
could promise me redemption,
I might put my grief to sleep.

But I have hit upon the single loss
no preaching can relieve.

III.
RAINA

Art is the magic mirror you make to reflect your invisible dreams in visible pictures. You use a glass mirror to see your face: you use works of art to see your soul.

– George Bernard Shaw, *Back to Methuselah*

Seek and Hide, or, For Raina (#4)

I keep rewriting your rosebush signature
as if I could find you at its end.
I keep counting my devotions and your gestures,
I count your steps and your intentions

until I reach a hundred, and then set off
tearing through imagination's mansion,
opening chests, the door beneath the stairs,
pulling back the curtains in the bedrooms.

But I could play hide and seek with you all day,
and never find you: for we are so alike,
that if I sought you, you'd be seeking, too,
and if I hid, we'd both be giggling in the closet.

I can examine you only as much
as my own body in the absence of a mirror.
Yes, this navel's singular, these hands
and feet are doubled as expected.

But what does it look like
on the backside of my skull? What colour
are my eyes? What grows there
between my shoulder blades?

Poem to Give to Sergius

The Bulgarians came down like a meteor bright,
As sleek but more bold than a panther at night;
Their sabres were raised up like slivers of moon,
Catching the shards of the rare afternoon,
Undaunted, unfearing, though they did not know
The black mouths of the guns were nothing but show;
Having been sent the wrong cartridges, their enemies
Would have otherwise thought them a handful of peas—

                oh, hang it.

Raina's Poem: To a Photograph

Go with him. Along November roads
Whitening to winter, he will go,
His poor form hunched against the pressing cold,
The tightened light, the fraying wet outside,
The hunger fraying from within.

Go: the coat will hug him through the war,
And when he puts his hand into the pocket
I hope more than his fingers will be warmed.
Be his companion on the tramping paths,
And talisman in battle when the air
Is bullet-riddled and explosion-gashed.
And though I know he'll keep himself more safe
Than I have power to do—if I could wrap
Him in my angel so the shots would see
How even enemies take care of him—
If I could make a semblance of my heart
And copy of my spirit, in the way
This picture mimics my mere face's shapes,
Or if I could fit myself inside his pocket,
I'll be sworn, I'd leap in there myself.

O be to him the sail to that old coat's
Battered bark, that has the honour now
To bear him on the ocean of the months!
O be my heart and hope itself, since this
Bodily container is too small
To contain their universal width.
What matter if my soul be squeezed into a page,
Since recently it clamours to break out?
What matter if my body be a shell
If he'll carry you, my heart, inside his coat?
And if he loses you, or leaves you, say:
My soul's been lost within the ruin of the world.

To Ellen, from Raina

I caught you in the windowpane,
looking just like me. You have the same
regal hair and overworking eyebrows
and cheekbone architecture that allows
a tent of freckles to stretch over.
But you look fainter, paler: so much paler!

Poor pale girl!
I know your frail material
will abide by its old curse:
though I am older, you will perish first.

After the Last

Raina.
Since you surprised my soul out of my lips,
and I turned, minutely capable of cataloguing
the basic shape of your receding form,

this house, this life, has set its haunches down
like some fantastic creature long extinct.
I walk around as if inside a firescreen
decorated with dead birds and butterflies.

But where you are holds no more reality.
I imagine you inside your carriage,
turning your warm gaze on the shifting scenery,
shifting into—what?
My imagination becomes as flat as maps.
I know there are mountains in your country,
but the space between them melds
as if they were painted on a page;
conjectured trees seem like carvings,
the sun looks like a clock.

In the face of an unguessable reality
which has perhaps existed all this time
along the edges of the treelines,
the gossiping of light within the leaves,
the edge of air that contains the flame
that only makes a halo for the wick,
a truth that keeps the world's unfolding layers
circling round each other like rings in trees—
confronted with this truth, all places
conjectured and perceived, seem
like the abodes of dolls.

My body moves amid these tapestries of air,
amid the elaborate lethargy of time,
but my irrepressible excess of heart
races after him, like the jewel moon
and streaming sun go tearing
through the horizon viewed
by his carriage window,
and though each day seems an age of man,
the march of minute centuries will end,
and in a fortnight he will return
and snap time like a matchstick in his hand.

Ellen.
No:

       not ever:

he will not return, that
is the last sight,
his disappearing back,
my eyelashes flung wide
before your vision dies
in the gulf of black.

Smacking hands
flutter up like a cluster
of startled birds.

Smile, though the first kiss
is continually the last.

Smile, though I have lost
the hub, the root, the pin
of my own life.

Smile, though the hopeful girl,
her lover, and her family
all died within the bombing
of an electrician's blink.

Smile: imagine all the smiling faces
are like the light within the trees,
the dream the streetsounds or the clink
of the windowblind wake you from,
that can never been recovered,
no matter how many times you go to sleep.

IV.
MARY

*I feel my heart glow with an enthusiasm which
elevates me to heaven, for nothing contributes so much
to tranquillize the mind as a steady purpose—
a point on which the soul may fix its intellectual eye.*

– Mary Shelley, *Frankenstein*

Epistles to Mary

i.

O child of light, how can I
write for you, clustered as you are
in your own words, your brain shaken
by genius when you were seven
years my junior,
its progeny

reverberating still, how can I
not write when you are the apex
of my days, when all the stumbling
action of my life coalesces in being, writing
for you? —and at least this fact of paradox
is my Romantic tie.

ii.

Once, I merely thought: Mary,
will you bless me?

And on the instant, chills ran up
my spine's lightning stick
as if I were a Shelleyan experiment.
Tears condensed upon my cheek.

O Mary, I know that you will bless me
along both the avenues
I've drilled out through my skull
to have traffic with the universe.

Invocation: To Mary

When I happen on my face, I mutter 'Mary,'
since now within myself I see her first,
or since I wish that I could see her clearly
beyond all compounded accolades on earth.

Mary, I lay down in my bed like Shelley
waiting in the churchyard for a ghost.
Although I know that you will ultimately
make me more corporeally whole,

I still search each scrap of air
for errant pieces of your soul,
since, even more than any other character,
their visitations to me a golder shine than gold,

I wish you'd bring your benediction down.
You make me strain all my superlatives,
already grasping as the minutes drown,
already terrorhearted that you'll leave.

For Mary

I give you my illogical fear of the water,
the beast whose body is the deep,
whose bristling fins are waves,
whose unfathomable stomach terrifies.

I give you the feeling that my father's skull
has such an altitude that it's almost obscured
by the clouds of his own genius.

I give you my worship of your husband,
not the play, not the actor, your husband actual.
I have loved him since I was your age,
his words set bellvibrations in my head
as if I already knew them. I love him
for the need for some to Hear
that penetrates two hundred years.

I give you the familiarity and the frustration
of the crouched handanimal
stumbling on the tundra of the page.
I give you my need for it,
the needle and the medicine.

I give you my art-exile,
my life like a carriage wheel
stuck sometimes in the mud.
And I give you, despite all my need
for moonphasing change, a wish
for a country house, a doting poet,
children in white smocks.

I give you my own tendency to be seasick,
literal as well as metaphorical.

I give you my comprehension
of all the strength required
and all the strength you have
to hold a man who disappears
within your arms' circumference,
because he is also fireworks of joy.
From other circumstances I also know
how to be compelled by a man
who holds another woman
in his other hand.
I give this to you too.

I give you too the haunting
of another woman's ghost seated
on the nightstand, the sense
that you bartered all your angel
for a man whose sight keeps slipping
from behind his eyes, and no
matter how he tells you you've done nothing,
the ghost still swings its heels
against the drawers of your bureau,
still slides its unsmell body down the hall.

And I give you the time jealousy
came up like a shark from my own depths
and ate my organs with its unblinking eye.
I feel that fire poker come up every time
I hear he is with Claire,
those devils stamping on my spine.

And I give back what you gave, the dream
I had before I travelled here to Utah's Alps,
that I unlocked a castle's mysteries
with Shelley and Lord Byron, found
a book of lapis lazuli preserved inside a crypt,

and brought it back into society, that manyheaded beast
that judged Shelley's treatment of me as unfair.
I loved him all the more, ferociously demonstrated
that I loved Shelley and would have no other.
So I bade him lay upon my lap
along a couch of maroon velvet with clawed feet,
and nestled his head into my elbowcrook
as if he were a baby. I loved him in explosion.
As I gazed upon him, his face's skin
began to pull back from his nostrils
and his lips, he became a leering sleeping monster
—but I loved him all the same. The skin melted
from his cheeks, it all pulled back until I held
nothing but a skeleton, but dreaming
I did not perceive the change
and simply loved him, loved him, loved him.
Not until I woke did I know the horror,
and not until I woke did I see that I was you.

I give you the fear that I might never be a mother,
even if I give birth.

And I give you the most compendiously personal
poem I've ever scratched up from the paper.

Sonnet: The Painted Eye

The penultimate time I looked upon my Shelley
as he said he never was attached to that great sect,
I gazed upon his radiance with such fixity
that when I turned my eyes upon that vast of black,
the gentle deep where swim the silver creatures
of the audience's eyes, I saw a Shelley made of light
imprinted on the surface of those waters,
flitting to the location of my sight.
Though I know my eyes' science only
burned on the image of that light-toned ghost,
it seemed the angel Mary prayed for finally
descended after centuries in that glowing host;
and this seeming visitation to his pining wife
shook, for me, the painted veil called life.

No Adonais

Like those poets, this show too
died within its bloom of youth,
before the Week Four doldrums come,
those nights, when despite all efforts
the pupil of the actor's eye
slips within its disc.

Some things die of old age,
but others die of youth.
Call the cause of death consumption,
a Grecian fever, or an ocean,
or all the electricians
taking down its suns.

In the end, death is best described
by the one-eyed triplets
cutting lengths of thread,
and one must choose a life lived,
or potential's power sealed.

The play remains inviolate.
Its death mask strives up, smooth
skin into smooth clay, the final answers
more like final questions,
its strength unfully tapped.

The Triumph of Death: For Mary

If ever Death
picked one for his bridewife
sisterdaughtermother
since once he fed a goddess
from a pomegranate ventricle,
it was you.

Your mother, from your own
placenta plucked out by unclean
fingers, shivered, sweated into death.

Her first daughter dozed with laudanum
into a thickened twilight.

Your husband's first wife
made a violent cradle from the Serpentine
for her third unborn baby and herself.

Your first baby girl did not revive,
as you dreamed, through rubbing by the fire.
She died of two weeks in the world,
she died of only thirty weeks
since being beaded in your womb.

Your second daughter died of a blurred Italian countryside,
Clara's namesake your husband's greater care.
Alone, in the hallway of an inn, while you waited
for Shelley to return with a physician,
her mouth's convulsions ceased.

Your first son, four whole years alive and at your side,
but only nine months since your second daughter died,
convulsed too into silence.

Shelley's poems on this event similarly falter
always into a silence
silent as the little Roman grave.

You thought then Death had won.
You could not unprise its fingers even with the birth
of your second son, so sunstar of your life the first had been.
And so frozen then that when life bled
out of your body's o, the only
thing that held your own life in was ice.

But The Triumph of Death was not finished

until the Bay of Spezia erased
your husband's body, its waters and its fish,
the final conflagration taking
everything but his unburning heart.

You were left with a child and a journal for a friend,
and only begged its mortallywhite pages
that Death, your motherhusbandchild,
would finally become you too.

V.
SHAKESPEARE

Sweet are the uses of adversity

– As You Like It

Stratford

Approaching the grave, we saw
a man kneeling at the railing.
For a moment I thought that he was praying,
but he was only photographically checking off
the bones encloasèd of a famous man.

But if I knelt, my prayers could only be
to an Unknowable. You, o the quintessence of
my fraternally twinned loves,
have disappeared. You scattered
into a million printed letters.

Out of this frustration,
or on the simple speculation of classist bastards
that no one but a lord of court could have produced
the masterworks of English, these images imprinted
on our subconscious minds, the invention of psychology,

they have tried to strip you of the glory
of your flat body that fans in turning pages,
to kick you from the honor of your grave.
They have tried to dig the dust,
but they do not listen to the placement of your tomb.

You are buried just below the altar,
with all your sons-in-law in row,
revered for simply marrying your daughters.
Would a mere player be buried in such state,
where anyone who kneels to God kneels to your bones, too?

This does not seem the grave of one incapable,
but proud and humble as the greatest artists are.
No courtier could write such kings and slaves

in the roundness of their humanities and minds,
no nobleman could be so regal yet so democratic.

Would a Lord have stooped to please the crowd,
and so please crowds centuries ahead?
Would he deign to understand a player?
And would a Lord have known his actors so,
have changed his Fools to Armin after Kempe went dancing off?

They do not know poets who do not know
they're made from what they lack, caulking up
their lives' holes with words.
Only some true human cipher could pull out
more multitudes than any besides God.

For this reason no sympathetic magic clings around the Birth-
    place,
Stratford is just bones.
You have been lifted up into your words.
And I rise closer to you in America, or wherever
my mouth resounds around your disintegrated pen,

wherever an entire mind is made of lines.
I say none of this to deify an author,
but to acknowledge God
in the theatre is the playwright,
pouring life in through the skull.

For this I have bent the knees of my heart
and said: You are more worthy of my body
than I am. Come.
And said: My self is only a character I play
for want of any other.

And so who cares if you are you,
or who you are? Your fame lies in your diffusion
into a thousand punctuations of the Light.
You are honored because you carried a crowd
inside, not just a man.

I have knelt to your soul
a thousand times, but not your bones.
You are not here,
but are blowing around the globe
as fast as speech.

The Juliet Chronicles

This is no great poet.
I gave and received my words
to and from the greatest, so I know.
Not because she writes, but because she knows
how I tuck my hair behind my ear,
I have given her my circlet of stars.

i. *My Love.*

When I first heard him speak, I knew he was
the purpose of my life. O strange order
of the pieces of my girlhood, now
winding into reason, my thread of years
turning on his spool, and his on mine,
double-turning, double-pulling in a kissing eight.
All that I am is distance, power drawn
from the pull of emptiness's horses.

ii. *Names.*

I wound myself in the curtains
and in this secret tent
breathed steam upon the windowpane
in which to write his name.

His name stayed longer there
than when I traced it in the water basin,
but still the R was fading
by the time I got to o.

This was only practice for new boldness:
to write his name over every inch of paper
I could find, the letters feathered
or hammered into jewels.

How dangerous to have papers with
his name beneath my mattress!
I will need to burn them
before we are married.

Which will be soon I hope.
And I stuck all with rosemary and Romeo,
and have discovered I always had
an M lined into my palm, a fated Montague.

What's in a name? I have lied.
Names give form unto eternity.
O me: I hear the far-off birth
of light from dark inside that sound.

   iii. *My Cousin.*

When we were children,
Tybalt would pull my hair, and hide behind
the tapestries and jump out as I passed.

But also when I broke a washbowl
he said he'd done it, and told me after
that he was already in so much trouble
for breaking boughs by climbing in the orchard
that it hardly mattered.

We have lost those languages, or else
we still have no other.

iv. *Ancient Damnation*

With my face plastered in the mask
of coarse brown apron, I should have heard
the devil's machinery within.

I should have known the prophecy
of genesis, the opening scene,
in all the carpet of foreshadowing,
the wormwood on the dug.

v. *A Dream of Death.*

Veil I never had
when I ran through the streets
drops upon me in the dream.
I wear the finest wedding gown of black
to attend the pomegranate feast.

A knight whose visor is a leer
lifts me to his bony horse
whose teeth grin round the bit,
and we ride through the dripping wood,
the muffled space between inky trees.

We come upon a grove where all the images
of these three days are milling,
the raven bearing snow
and dove's feathers like an olive in its beak,
the lamb with the muzzle of a wolf,
the scissors of the stars,
the mandrakes striding on their rooty legs,
animated saints of stone, their carved eyes staring,
and in the middle, I see my own body standing

in a white nightdress in a flash of lightning
holding a red rose to my breast.

And the earth opens, Phaeton's chariot
racing into night, and the last,
the exclamations of my body's upflung arms.

The cathedral chiselled from the middle of the earth
takes over both my selves.
The candles burn cold smoke.
The bodies assembled
in the pews that reach into dim vanishment
shake their shrouded heads
as I crunch the petals of the aisle,
attended by a train of Tybalts.
My ancestors as priests
keep pulling their flesh back on their skulls.
The altar is a tomb.

But this is not the dream of death.
I do remember—
the face that floated in its paleness
as if it would fix into that shape
forever—I do remember—
well where I should be

in this always waking
to discover, without variation,
the body on the other side,
the earth's worst horror,
the inevitable perpetual loss.

That slice of his dead body
is the dream, and at the daggerpoint
I wake, the point the blade the hilt

what lamb what lady why bride
gently shaking me awake.

    vi. *After.*

On earth we think
the stars can love and hate.
But when that sphere is broken
and we ascend each level,
the stars become the floor, and we see them clearly
fixed in smiling, only smiling,
placid brainless smiles.

On earth we preserved
the flame of love mid-leap,
and they will say, for all our grief,
it never faded.

But heaven is the stuff of preservation.
Immortality is standard, and it douses
the power of our earthly reach,
when we lie entwined, dissolving to each other
on the washed lawns of the hereafter.
I pick oranges and cakes from unlabouring trees,
and feed my love's slaked mouth,
and chide him, Left me to die
by dagger, while you took the pleasant wine
of gentle death? It is much better to die
by poison than by knife.
He returns, How do you know?
I have done both, I say.
Aren't you special?
You made me believe you thought so.
And he: Well, at the time, I thought you were dead!

What was I supposed to do?
Listen to your dream, perhaps? I answer.
What silly kind of lover would listen to a dream?
—but he is grinning. So goes our love
the way of all true loves,
smiling placidly.

And because he is by me when I write
with my finger in the sands of heaven,
stripped of images and verbs, I say:
Eternity is only in the briefest things,
and all that lives forever does not live.

Eating Verse

You must throw yourself upon it like a sword
of air and secret fire, and die
for a while, more rapidly.

You must launch yourself into the approaching wave
and incorporate into the ocean.
Your gut must be the fireblanket

for the detonating word, your eyes the wells
into which God drops
the reflected moon.

The Five Acts of Lady M

O power, like an approaching hoofbeat sounding
devouring the stillness of the unseen road:
come like you say come
make my blood thick,
make it riverfast.

O power, I know you're tapped
into the lifeveins of the earth,
and its ore is not avarice,
but love. But if ignored?

O power, I know your tragedy
is the gradual diminishing
of your voice until

your power wristbled or jumped
into a final oh, oh, oh

into tomorrow, and tomorrow, and tomorrow.

The Diana Chronicles

i.

The casement is shut,
but the songs still permeate the wood.
Every night he comes with musics of all sorts,
and sings while standing on the greenblack grass,

and feeling like I'm sitting in my skull,
I sit inside the shuttered room,
with music seeping from another sphere.
I wish I were an insect or a mote

who could speck down on the windowsill
with no hurt thought of my watching him,
no hurt conceivable from my tiny wings.
I wish I were my birdheart, full

invisible, who can do no hurt
so long as it stays absent from my chest.
But, being human, in the morning I will go
into the garden and wonder where he stood.

ii.

I maintain my goodness
so that filth will not advance
further in the world
by the borders of my body.

So it was spoken truly
that my body's like a statue in the park,
the surface and the core the same immobile substance,
still amongst the beating of the trees.

iii.

After he'd
downshaken me
like the contents of a box,

I could not speak a word,
for fear my lipbow
would let the arrows of his swearings out,

and she'd fall down slain
by the anti-Eros, knowledge.
I do not envy her,

whose heart is sharpened
by rubbing on her ribs.
I could only hold out

the ring, as if to quote myself
inside its o. I wanted to say
I am glad that it is you.

but feared I'd also add
because I would not want to be between
such lying and the sheet.

iv.

When I go into my chamber, the bed
and dresser seem to stand apart,
the walls draw back and hold their breath,
the new sheets that my mother laid
are stretched and white as death.

The night before, the furniture
quivered when she entered,
my own comb leapt within my hand,
the casement itself rippled
like a wishstone in a pond.

v.

Let me trail you still, into the north,
over mountains, through the provinces
that expand like liquid spilled out of the roads.
I would split my shoulders
to make wings. I would crack my face
to eradicate the wrong I might have done.
I would gladly pry my skull where once
the musket of a pupil busted through
and left a ball still swivelling at the back.
I would gladly crow open my head if I could
extract that dry ball rattle out that follows me,
and ticks against your pious heels, all the way to France.

vi.

These litanies have carried me.
As the King comes closer by my steps,
I pinch my consciousness for boldness,
saying: *This is my life, this is my life.*

And as I cross the threshold, know
if I hold fast to my honesty, we all
kept Lambwhite in the night; if I fall,
dirt will swipe across three souls.

Kill the Boys

The last *Henry*, as I lay down on my bloody sheet,
my bloody rag scarfwise wound around my neck,
the gash made by slashing, three quarters up,
the blue jewel of my young male throat, the female skin intact:

I realised: I am dying indeed,
I am laying down into my death.

I closed the curtains on my Boy's *last syllable,*
and then performed the rite of rag and sheet,
knowing that he would *come no more, never, never...*
and then *All my mother came into my eyes—*

but either I cannot have a form to mourn,
or else no mourners at the funeral:
the corpse can't weep once dragged on stage,
the living twin buried dumb in its dead body.

Portia

I will not betray her secrets.
They will go with me to my final
unapplauded curtain.

Quite explicitly she asked me not to tell.
More than any that I have known
of Shakespeare's heroines,
she hides herself in riddles—
and when she finally unveils,
the wound of her modesty flinches at the air.

Of all her jewelled beauties,
her unremarked humility
is most luminescent
in the body's muffled dark.

But I will not tell, because we two
have travelled battered on two solestanding legs.
I will not tell, because I clutched her most
of any against the flood of space,
clutched her like a bundled baby
in the war-tattered town of her nativity,
clutched her like another's shoulder on a bomb-rocked ship.

For her I wept most and loved longest,
a cohabitation deeper than infatuation's flame.
She was more than love; at times
she was my life, when in the tar of midnight
we were confronted with the unsun
sides of our selves' satellites,
but in the horror of the blackened mirror
I found that her unhand and my own
were indistinguishable in the redundantly blind dark.

I will not tell—although there was a time
when I thought I could tell,
after I no longer depended on her daily lifting of me.

But I will not tell, although my eyes
dropped tears at my body dropping
from her grip. I cannot believe
that she has died,
having shared my body with her
since she was put in my Zeuslike womb
sixteen months ago.

Wound

i. *The Beginning*

Today when your Hotspur-doubled arm
wrestled me to the ground,
the gauntlet on your wrist
scratched my forearm a raw field
with one long catclaw line of red.

I did not notice it until Kate
undoubled me and left me
in the dressing room, putting up our hair,
when I saw my mirrored arm
and realised that sting
was something other than the usual.

ii. *The End*

Now I have as many scratches on my forearm
as I have fingers blooming from its end.
I wish they were tattooed into my skin,
so perfect a marriage mark they seem
between the actor and the character,
so much they seep of sex and power
that my life's slim circumference lacks,
homesick for my infinity's full track.

But the first of them has almost faded,
is only visible in certain angles of the light.
They last only slightly longer than Kate,
who will slip under the surface of the dated
days under which my own life is always slipping.
These scratches happened in a flash of feeling
like a character, but will leave me like a poem,
having written nothing half so ripping at skin's seam.

Lady Percy and I Attend a Dress Rehearsal

I watched Hotspur enter, bloodheaded,
arms ending in a sword, and thunderbolt
against the Prince of Wales.

No Lady Percy ever had to see her husband's
blade get knocked away, the messy fist
and elbow struggle cut off by the double
stroke, coating the sword with his insides,
the first stab that incapacitates, then
the second, his guts hugging for a moment
the steel of Monmouth's sword, which then removed
takes the same way all losses take.

In this hides the riddle of our doubling.
Hotspur's real Elizabeth and William Shakespeare's Kate
never saw their husbands lose their lower legs and kneel,
who would himself have been enthroned upon that roan,
now coating his kneebones with the battlefield,
crawling, saying suddenly he could prophesy
who denounced the Welsh man's augury,

while I, never married to the man I watched,
was rattled violently by my shoulders
in the theatre's swamp of seats, coating
my nose and cheeks with tears,
feeling as if I were transmitting
the sight of his lifeless body
into Kate's universal mind,

and being the tearducts for her,
since hers are incorporeal, or else rotted
long before John and Mary Shakespeare
welcomed out their son the smith of English
crammed with his myriad humanities

the same bloody bawling way all are welcomed out.

Lady Percy, bound onto the wheel of loss,
continually supplicating her husband not to go,
continually losing the battle as he leaves,
wrestling him in Wales, and after the great gulf
that subdivides the story, showing up as briefly,
left continually with nothing but her bravery.

I'm glad I'm not so fettered to that wheel,
whose fore-end is always falling to the dirt,
but for several years it seems
I too am continually losing
sometimes without possessing much to start,
continually left with just that same
invisible companion of my courage.

Which is worse, that like mountain-bound Prometheus,
the organ of your love regrows
to be plucked out again each time it dies?
Or that I should lose my heartpocket's contents
from its coat of holes, sewn up by a needle
with no thread, lose even your loss
in the maze of space
and in the barricades of weeks eventually
lose the rinds and fruit until the stones
of this emotion only rattle, dwindle
and leave me finally like a reed
taken from a lake?

Suffice that I supplicated, lost, and now I weep
for your husband, cradled in stage blood.
As usual, I possess no answer
to that paradox of doubling:
Which of us is marching in whose coats.

Helena

With your coronation
I am coming into my power

but only as the uncrowned king is nothing
until he leaps to meet its round.

Years of grailing you at distances
now illuminate my faults.

Your sanctifying star lies so far above
my heart's earthslogged altitude

that I must not damage you
by making you like me

but I must bend my dull self up
to fit your merit in.

VI.
ACTORS

I labour by singing light
Not for ambition or bread
Or the strut and trade of charms
On the ivory stages
But for the common wages
of their most secret heart.

– Dylan Thomas, "In My Craft or Sullen Art"

Acting

We make a lace of spaces don't we?
I make arson from an electric candlestick,
you pull the Cambridge courtyards out of words,
I pick up your syllables from the venerated air,
we discover double functions for a hand,
you lash a raft of it, I write romance in a palm,
we construct lives out of sentences,
love out of bodies.

For

Not for the audience I act
though I'm pleased when they enjoy,

nor for directors in the house's black—
though their guidance I employ;

not for note—fickle! —or fame—a fluke!
—or for my welcome pay;

my reward is that onyx jewel
in the other actor's eye.

Actor to Actor

Come meet me on the crossroads of the dawn,
where the horizon is the colour of a wing,
dim and pale as the doorframe of sleep,
smooth as the doorknob of death.

Come meet me where the dust is sifting up
from the roadways of reality and dreams,
where their gravel makes a heart an x,
and the plains are replicating grass

into infinity. Order is overrated. Come
and with an agile twisting of your fingers,
tear up the root of circumstance, and make
a crater where the roads were once defined.

Romeo

When I remember you
              you are in blue,
       you are turning

and looking up at
me   you
are stuck in these loops
like film on a spool

when it was the
external, not the   internal
world that was against us.

It is your broad love that is scissors.
You know this.   I know
this. I took it anyway.

I have not seen you for a day.   No,
less. Pointlessness
enlarges time.
O by this count   I

I sit in front of the paper fire
and lay my arms across
the landscape of the couch,

and remember you turning
and the little things like the way
you kissed   the inside of my elbow.

Parallel Arcadias

I knew you in another life.
Once I kneeled on chairs and flung my birdhands
in tight alphabets of gesture,
and you heard the selfsame words I said
and responded with the words I heard.

But when you played him, how pacing
was your scholar's walk?
Did you punctuate like the baton of a conductor
with a single upturned finger?

And when I loved that man, how much
did you let that young girl in? It's as if
we are both leaning towards a wall
of mirrors and tapping on the silver.

Is it because that life was my yet greatest love,
that now, in this other alternate reality,
you glance at me so fiercely and so tender
that my bloodmuscle bores a hole in my back ribs?

Love Triangle

I will not lie and say I loved him for you:
he clearly keeps the instigating flint within him,
as all who know him love him as inevitably
as Newton's apple drops down from the tree.

But I do go up to the gallery for you,
and prick open my heartwound by watching him,
which means that I inevitably love,
my own forktongue tempting my own Eve.

And I will continue slicing up heart's fruit for you,
to garner greater honesty by double-loving him,
inevitably pulling me down to my knees
as sky-laden Hercules in the Garden of Hesperides.

Voice and Unvoice

We sat in the backyard brickwalled
with the ivy draped and tapping
against the redness of the brick,
and the sun sat in the ivy, on the wall,
and the sky spilled its liquor liquid-blue
into the wide rim the world's glass,
and best of all universal, you

spoke in Shakespeare,
learning lines of verse,
while I followed in the white playworld bible
of the script, collecting the invisible
words petalled from your lips
and comparing them to the eyewise lace
the black words make from a white page,

and periodically distracted, you
would point out wild strawberries
and treesized weeds and birds
within the garden, and periodically distracted, I
semicoloned my eye sideways from the script,
continually scissored by your beauty,
attempting to find an imperfection

to make all the beauty somehow bearable,
the breeze, the sun, the ivy and the wall,
the May, the blue, the bodies of the words,
the white paint flaking from my wooden chair,
the wine of Shakespeare poured and pouring
into the exquisite vessel of your self and borne out
on the sightless mortal angels of your breath,

not mountains or cathedrals are as beautiful as that,
the perfect poet living in the body
perfect, painfully, swimming in the rich
sungleamed river of your voice,
and the insubstantial thread that sutures closed
our once-opened spoken love
back into my silent silenced flesh.

This Life Denies Us

This life denies us
even perfect sadness.
The rock remains uncut,
the gem of many facets
submerged within the roughness.

Sometimes it seems alleviation,
life's comedy continually intruding
to help out those who feel.

This dichotomy is life's truth predominant,
as the master playwright knew,
the Clown who carries in the asp,
the Capulets' servants who don't know
they're blundering among youth's fatal fireworks,
Falstaff popping up beside the noble Percy slain.

I am trying to construct the final couplet
that you dropped,
trying not to break up my lines to weep,
but finding that life's text
is often just its sobs,
no iambs but the heart's relentless hammering,
no rhymes besides the mirror held
to a monarchic line of disappointments.

After the War

You brought armistice
when we stood in the theatre housing hallway,
firstkissing tentative as trees.

Now, well over two years later,
which is centuries in the eight generations
of characters who have lived here,

with their longshort memories
(never knowing this same thing happened
the same way on their yesterdays),

those factions that once warred
not only coexist but intermarry, their children's
biracial opalescent skin a blend of life and art.

Unacting

This is a fatal profession.
I seek anything that gives a hit
of honesty into the veins. I
set my spine up like a lightning rod.

For this reason wilfully with forethought
I build a room inside my body
where I love you utterly.
There will be no impropriety:
the door will not be opened to that room;

but I take its curtains with both my hands
and wring them out and lay them
on my eyelids before sleep.
Nothing pleases theatre's gods
like striding in the monster's cave
with no armour and no sword.

Of course I throw myself into the fire.
If I had some closer, more expensive thing
I'd pitch that in instead.
But I must serve
as my own virgin sacrifice.
I am my own chestdug heart
fed skyward to the gods.

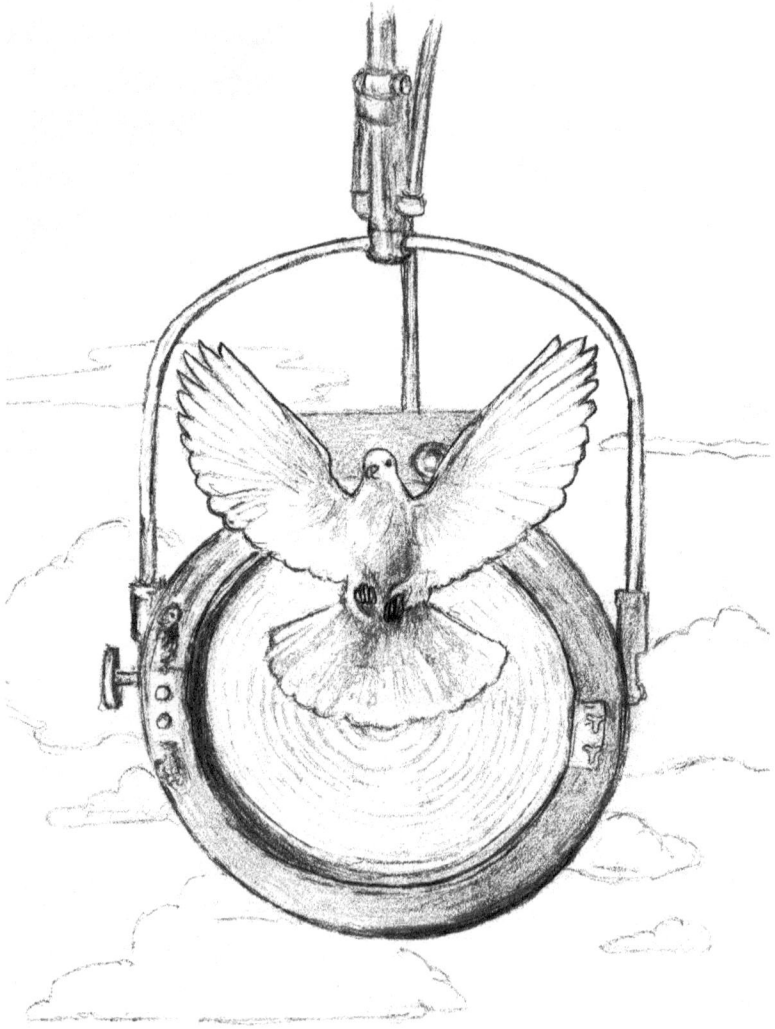

VII.
AN ACTOR'S LIFE

When such as I cast out remorse
So great a sweetness flows into the breast
We must laugh, and we must sing,
We are blest by everything,
Everything we look upon is blest.

– William Butler Yeats, "A Dialogue of the Self and Soul"

Thanks-giving in the Theatrechurch

I am so Godblest blessed
in this pack of lives
the theatre gives me
that I could ask no greater destiny
than a future where this bounty luck
does not make me pay it back
with misfortune's equal sum.

But I know I am not the cause of my success.
You ancient wheel, if you'll spare your turning,
I will ride up with a humble heart
and teeter at the zenith.

Paradox

i. *Thought*

If I could think myself
into a revelation,
I would sit upon a stone
and set my stonelike skull
into the basin of my hands
until my hair caught fire
or my forehead bloomed.

But our capability unlaces
if too much thought is fixed upon
the mechanics of the acting plane.
To think is death
upon the stage's battlefield,
where nothing but a vulnerable helmet
will save us in the end.

ii. *Joy*

If I could weep myself
into a consolation,
I'd plant my eyes into the earth
like tulip bulbs, and wait for them
to spring up with a recompense for loss.

But all things fade, all
lovely things large enough
to found the heart on
derive half their loveliness
from their unwakable mortality.

Theatre Sickness

He says he is a slave
to theatre. I too
am that sad slave, tending,
spiteful eyed in the oiled gutters,
hands like lopsided spiders,
snuffling for a fix, starving
in the bloodshot morning.

That withdrawal
would make me haunt my life:
my cheeks scraped hunger-sunken, my mouth
leering toward the grin of skeletons,
the jaw cut slack and smacking like a ghost,
this image hunching around the image of my body,
testing every rib and finger for escape,

puppetting the external theatre, pulling up
the curtains on a smile
where the throat begins
to hollow.

Selfcentred Aria

This waitress, who serves me,
or I who am to be served,
what can I know of her, or she
of me? She is Bit-Part: Waitress
in my novel, and I am Bit-Part: Customer (with sandwich)
in her movie: *Alison the Waitress*, or, more likely,
Alison, in whose dramatic and comedic exploits
waitressing does not figure highly.
As customering does not in mine.
But so we serve each other.

I would sing from your eyes, if I could.
But I would have to guess, presume from ponytail
and make nametag inferences. My presumption
is that people hate presumptions:
the defensive you-don't-know-me.
Is it worse to leave you a lifeless waitress-doll,
or worse if the customer-doll assumed
to construct for you imagined life
so less spiderwebbed and intricate
than the one you truly have?

Somehow I can't put away frustration
that I will never get a pass to see the world
exactly as the one beside me sees it;
I'll always look through these imbalancing binoculars.
No matter how old I get, this simple fundamental
of existence that we all grasp at early ages
still waggles like nosethumbed fingers,
smarts like sticks and stones.

from Song of the Young Poet

Today I hugged my battered arm
through all the hours, where yesterday
they scraped the infection from pulsing bone.
My hand is bandaged like a thought
without words: I do not know
how much hole there is below
those stratospheres of gauze.

I could not look, I felt them scrape away,
I could not look but stared
at the plugs on the wall: color-coded
blue then red then grey,
and again, again repeated as a whispering appeal:
"To His Heart, Bidding it Have No Fear": *Be you still.*

Today I knelt and prayed in the testing church
of an audition: a practice stripped of ceremony
(what art thou, thou) in the blank and slumping hallway,
but a religion of tradition, embodying the history,
the wine and bread of poetry,
Shakespeare descending from the universal passion,
to make my body into the worded incarnation.

The faces of those who guard the places of the play
like somber priests, regarded me familiarly:
blue then red then grey.
You read well, said they. Their coldness imposed
the disparity of speech and thought upon the room
where I'd exhumed the saddened Desdemona,
where I'd been conduit for the current of emotion
that briefly visits and inhabits like a god inside a temple.
I left unfrozen, unafraid; after all: *Him who trembles.*

Today I met the Poet, for whom
every written and unwritten thing
I have written or not written
to deliver to such brilliance.
Theatre is communion,
but poetry is a lonely enterprise,
writing against the whiteness
that presses at the end of days.

On the black afterwards sidewalks
my swagging legs rebelled
and I fell onto a doorstep,
not moving, muttering:
The lonely majestical multitude.

Today I returned and examined the shapes
of my face in the old flopped liar,
and thought, What if I wrote
a book of my life, my whole life,
all of it fitting into today?

I fumbled with the faucets in elation,
watched the water which ran beneath my hands.
I had to sleep and wake before the realization
cracked that it had been done before.
The day was destined
to be part of a larger poem,
and nothing more. *Cover over and hide.*

Belief

Opposing trains roared past me on their tracks,
like serpents swallowing their tails along the planet's disc,
like the monster coming for Andromeda
chained to her train station bench, and they rattled a
percussion in my skullbone until it sounded silver,
and I thought O what monsters!
if I did not know they are mechanical
and could only kill
unfeeling—o what wonder
is daily killed beneath the boots of hours.

I tricked and tricked my sense into belief
and walked to the platform's edge to feed myself
into its many mouths with all my
blood-bones ringing in my bravery.

O fragment of my mind a halfchild still!
I feed you this, you sweet emotional animal!
How long may I deceive you that you hold
puppets whose straw could spin to gold?

Tomorrow and Tomorrow and

Of what significance is this I
I haul around, but a life to snuff
in the absence of a closing curtain, a brief
story structured undramatically?

I spend so much time
bending all my strength into the birth
of a fullgrown human, a rhyme
of fiction's ejaculate and truth,

I am almost not surprised to look askance
upon my self like some strange dinosaur
passed fantastically out of existence.
I almost expect some day to make a door

through which I will step into a being
utterly different: such as, a man with brown eyes
that slide under his hat, and children clustering
at the close of day with faces like a field's fertilities.

The Year of Roving Approaches

i

When I miss you for an hour,
I miss you for a year, like sleep
as an experiment for death.

ii

Where I need theatre
is like a hole dug for a sapling
and accidentally plowed through to the Chinaside of the earth.

iii

Watching others audition
for the family I leave behind,
their mouths become like those of fish.

iv

I promised the director I would not tell you
about the auditions, likened it to a knight
falling in a battle for his king.

But instead I feel that I've betrayed
you, chosen art before love
once again.

v

A year of touring plays: the difficulty
as though each night we had to find
a dry pit to coax the fire in.

The journey: images of pilgrimage
flash up: fire projections on the tentflap,
the texture of the desert stretching

underneath the infinite black palm,
the days rocked on a camelfooted sway,
the bright colours only on our clothes.

vi

But such endeavour on the path of art
is desert and monsoon, grassbitten passes
through the snowhigh mountains, the temperate

and junglewild forests both wet and dripping, all
demanding that you camp your soul
where they dew lays down, gets in.

vii

It is my fault.
I bashed in the windows of my house,
and waved the rifle of a year

at the headholding shoulderhunch
of my family and love. They will live
on independent,

while I trudge the white lanes
in the black night with the gun
of my ambition clanking.

x

And you my best loved personal god
of theatre, my calendar of life,
how can I know my mouth

will not one day fumble,
how can I distinguish skill from habit,
when I don't know what

it is I do, or how
it's done at all?
It's like analysing the air inside the lungs.

xi

And like a truly ancient god
its legtrunk shakes the wooden earth,
rattling the pebbles and the silhouettes

of the terse black leafless trees
and puts in the tornado of its mouth
the children of all my other preferences.

xii

But what am I
to be worthy: I am nothing.
I have no teacher

but myself. What have I ever done
to deserve a droplet of the rain
this god has Aprilled down

around my widesprung eyes,
my flungback brow,
my arms like sails?

from Two Affirmations

I dreamt they took a section of the population
to killing camps to die.
I did not know, or do not now recall
what our offence was, that the earth must be
unburdened of our lives.

But for weeks I skirted, wary of the streets,
a squinting vigilance flattening my eyes.
Every gesture, and each piece of trash,
and every evening skyline,
I collected as my last.

When I was called up, terror
mingled with relief.

Endless winding lines, bureaucratic buildings,
yellow-lit waiting rooms, paperwork. Dying
had become as difficult as life.

The camp itself was not so terrible.
Everyone had their own weakspringed cot
and woollen blanket, and white
too-sweetsmelling sheets.

I claimed one with my satchel, meditated
on whether they would find my notebooks and computer
and burn all I'd ever written, burn my mortal angel,
or if they'd have the luxury to care.
But even if I were a better writer,
I knew my sheer obscurity
would make my body's death
my utter death indeed.

I came across a friend inside the camp, the man
I played opposite in *Pygmalion*. His pants
were torn off at his calves like a shipwrecked sailor.
I have been here three months,
he said, So I am likely to live
about another month.

He seemed cheerful as one could be
with that sentence as a fact.
But what life is life inside a box,
its lid nailed shut?

But as I looked at death as a thing
as close and absolute as the coming of the spring,
and life until then stripped of productivity,
I thought: I have loved profusely,

I was given many friends and lovers worthy of profusion;
my parents have been good confidants and guides
every second since my birth,
and unflinching, unashamed I have followed
at the godheels of my dream: to have many human lives in one,

and I achieved the highest hope of any honest actor,
an entire year of service to my favourite playwright;
and though I did not see it to completion,
I had the strength before I died to win the prize
for which a thousand artists jousted.

And I performed Ophelia
in the broad mud walk that ran
between the bunkered buildings.

Seeing Children

Many lament that we forget
how to play, once we grow out
of (or shrink within) our childhood;
but even I, who for my life and bread
elaborately pretend, don't remember how to play
with any substance but emotion's clay.

Birthday

Today I become as old as Keats was
when he died. I will commemorate
this birthyear by playing Shelley's
wife. Though maybe Fanny would be more appropriate,
no one (to my knowledge) has written them a play.
A life in theatre lacks such self-determination.

I wildly celebrate this birthday
by travelling to New York to audition.
This is as appropriate for me
as words are for the objects they describe.
No finer fire could burn new age into my body
than the doves that bravery brings into the ribs.

I emerge, as always, beaming at the universal,
grinning at the man who runs the pretzel stand,
at anyone who'll catch my pupil,
flushed holywhole by impossibility's bright hand.

It also fits me snug as skin that I am travelling.
One year ago I wrote: My life is motion,
the unmossed stone— a phrase now right for hammering
above the only door I have, the one
framed above my eyes.
The excessive breadth of air is always blowing back
the smoke the human fire tries to rise
from spindly twigs in a campsite's dripping black.

Therefore believe the Myth of Travelling.
Believe the autumn leaves, in fish-like schools they go
down the open road, their dry feet clattering.
Believe the highway angel, the skipping moon his halo,
his robes of layered coats, his fingers like ignition keys,

his bootwings making gypsy music of the map,
his hair is like a river delta, but his iris colours freeze.

Believe the sky sits in the horizon's lap,
believe the earth lays down and lays down
and lays down beneath the reaching space;
believe that space becomes your lover then,
believe that space is your full nature's canvas.

Believe, because I've chosen the old
perfection of the work above the life;
my body's jewelled with all the stories it has told,
but lacking simple garments for itself.

Finally it's fitting that I wildly celebrate
this birthday by scratching up these words
from the paper's depths. What finer fire could inundate
my body with new age than the spirit birds
that writing releases from my fingers' cage.
We all need birth-days to have tradition,
to commemorate the layers of our age.
This writing's mine, art's old remuneration.

The Actress

i. *Island*

In your poem, you call me 'the actress.'
It resonates: yes, the rest of me
erased that I might be inhabited.

A fitting word: inhabited,
as if I were an island,
a fitting metaphor.

Odd the race that lives there,
in their storyhigh huts in the ropehung trees.
Mostly women, a few boys

peek out from the verdant green,
the rich multicoloured fruit they eat
heavy as organs on the branches.

Every year, several new people
materialise on the beach.
What country, friends, is this?

Whoever is the newest
is made Queen. All think
she has been sent by gods.

Some may be jealous,
some sympathetic tribefolk
may lend her gestures, tactics, hair.

But still on all sides
the sky melds into the ocean's flat,
the ocean's perfect merciless infinity.

ii. *The War of Life and Art*

I am an actress.
Not just in the physics of your poem,
but in all universes,

I have lost my name.
I lopped it off myself.
I am alone to blame.

This is what Art's Revolution
brings to the guillotine:
my own name bloody in the basket,

the rioting of ghosts
in the unpopulated streets,
all the facades of canvas,

the unmerciless stage flats.
I have misplaced my life.
I am myself to blame.

To Actors Shooting a Commercial

Do not look too hard upon those mansions
Or gaze on the expanse of dappled grass
Where you are paid to play the owners of
Unimaginable happiness.

See, but do not reflect much on the rooms
too numerous to be marked by life
(The same way I am picked to play a mother
Because my skin's as unstretched as my womb).

We are selected to display the faces
American prosperity should have
And thereby the opinions you should buy,
We, who survive by chewing stones, or when
We get it, language, the bootstrap of the soul.

So do not look too hard at those twin pools
In the backyard (the extra for the times
When one clear turquoise square is not enough)
Or the parade of clothes they tried on you,

But take your wages gratefully back home
To your city nest of sagging walls,
In case those who have ease must forfeit fire
That makes the majesty of heart create
A greater space in life's own raging skin.

Life's a Colander

Yet in this captious and intenible sieve
I still pour in the waters of my love
And lack not to lose still.

I've recently been thinking of the way
All's Well's Helena compares herself
To kitchen implements, because sometimes
When I look at you my sternum smarts
With an unromantic sledgehammerlike slam,
Or a pricking like the notching-in of nails.
If these sensations were not palpable,
I'd pick lighter metaphors than tools.
But carpentry's the best comparison.
Sometimes affection hits us like a pan.

And always, it seems, life's a colander.
I've repeated this poem's epigraph
In dozens of auditions, as I kneel
And pray in this same way and saying this,
And every time a genuine emotion
Pours through the little holes in o's and e's,
The sieve of Shakespeare never filling, too.

For in the end, I ride the gyroscope
Of this crazy stage-dependent life
Because I have a surfeit of my self,
And must dispense with all of it somehow.
This excess abundance is the reigning star
Of all I do, my too-much way of writing,
The bodily requirement that I make
More than one person from my single form,
And the atomic way my rib-bomb detonates.

Theatrechurch

i.

Death of my child who shares my body comes.
Autumn is a petticoat beneath the skirts of August.
O God in life and life in God,
like a trinity identical,
whose Name is pure semantics,
who is worshipped where the fibre-end
of love springs its hairlike root,
who is worshipped with a book
or with teeth flaring at the sky.

ii.

Against the simper of the sideways lioness
eating unborn children in the black age of her mouth,
I will make my fingers to a lance,
my veins into pins, and leave
my eyes and ribcage like tilled soil,
like the water's stretch of surface tension.
Forge this body from its own melted mould.
This is the life upon the lines,
the hardest stone to set to, being soft.

iii.

I take this, death inside a day's membrane,
a fan of lives within duration
of a sole mortality.
I take this, where the hourhand is fatal,
where the eveningline calls in the doves and fire.
Praise those fictions, but also praise the chase

that bleeds challenge on reality.
I build my time like a hut of sticks on the shore
of a hurricane delta. O my God: never give me ease.

ACKNOWLEDGEMENTS

For careful reading of my poems and offering thoughts and suggestions, I would like to thank my father, Henry Glassie, and my husband, Eric Gilde, who are both writers themselves. And of course I must acknowledge the tireless efforts of Zachary Bos at Pen & Anvil. To have had three such truly excellent writers give considered thought to allowing the volume to achieve its own aims has been this small collection's greatest boon.

I have many things for which to thank playwright and director Charles Morey, which include taking a chance on an utterly unknown and unseen young actor, but here, I am chiefly thankful for his time in reading this book and writing its truly lovely introduction.

The theater is founded on collaboration, and these poems would literally not exist had it not been for all of the people who directed, created, costumed, lit, constructed, and attended the productions mentioned herein. My greatest thanks go to the directors and producers who have hired me to play, and the directors and other actors who have inspired me to do the same.

Other actors are truly my favourite part of acting, the how and the why of my joy. I genuinely must thank every actor with whom I've ever had the privilege to work for the substance of this book; many were literally the inspiration for some poems, but all are implicitly part of their muscle and blood. I do not have space to name them all here, but I am grateful to every one of them.

In seeking the underlying cause of this whole habit of writing poetry, thanks must be given to Andrew Stauffer, a professor of mine at Boston University, who taught me to be as passionate about poetry as I always have been about the theater. The greatest and final thanks must also be given to both of my parents, Kathleen Foster and Henry Glassie, not only for my general upbringing (i.e., minus television, plus family outings to see Shakespeare), but also for teaching, by their own example, the importance of writing, reading, and scholarship of life. They are also to be credited for supporting my choice of an unstable, peripatetic profession, and not asking when I'm going to do something serious with my life.

NOTES TO THE TEXT

I. CHARACTERS

"To Eliza (Present)", p.25

This poem was written to Eliza Doolittle in Shaw's *Pygmalion*, my first show out of college. It is the first poem I wrote about a character. In the play, Professor Higgins teaches Eliza, a lower-class flower-girl, to speak properly with an upper-class accent, passing her off successfully as a 'lady.' Eliza is then stuck in a position of being neither a flower-girl, nor quite a genuine lady, which I refer to in the lines "which of us is me, / the changed or the original." There is a parallel between her transformation from flower-girl to lady and my transformation from Ellen to Eliza. "You know very well all the time you're nothing but a bully" is Eliza's reply to Higgins in Act IV.

» "Sonnet for Geoffrey," "Geoffrey's Riposte," "Hanging Out," "Actor/Actress", pp.28-31

I played Geoffrey Dunderbread in Amy Freed's farce about Shakespearean authorship, *The Beard of Avon*. Geoffrey is the boy in the Elizabethan troupe of actors who plays the female roles, as would have been the practice in those days; the original Juliet and Lady Macbeth would have been played by boys, as would have, more interestingly, the original Rosalind, thus creating the interesting scenario of a boy playing a girl playing a boy playing a girl. Though I was merely a girl playing a boy playing a girl, it was still an interesting challenge. I had actually played a couple of male roles previously, including Malcolm in a professional production of *Macbeth*, a slightly-androgynous Puck in two professional productions of *A Midsummer Night's Dream*, and Guildenstern in a college production of *Rosencrantz and Guildenstern Are Dead*. But the issue of playing a male role who, in most scenes, was wearing a female costume, made me more aware of needing to specify my physicality.

» "Lady Lettice's Poem", p.32

Lady Lettice was my other character in *The Beard of Avon*. Though there is little love lost between her and Queen Elizabeth, as depicted in the play, Lettice's main function is simply to be the female member of Elizabeth's court, which consists of only five actors, playing Lord Walsingham, Lord

Burleigh, Sir Francis Bacon, Henry Fitch… and Lady Lettice. However, this poem is not based on any scenario which appears within the play, but simply on my research into the facts of Lady Lettice's life, which are fascinating enough to spark interest in a pile of wet leaves. I will keep this as brief as possible, though I encourage you to look up all the juicy details, which would make the editors of *Us* magazine lament that nothing interesting happens any more:

Born Lettice Knollys, she was a grandniece to Anne Boleyn, thus related to Queen Elizabeth, and the two women were close from childhood. However, while Lettice's first husband, the Earl of Essex, was fighting in Ireland, she may have started a dalliance with Robert Dudley, Earl of Leicester (pronounced 'Lester'), who was a favourite of Queen Elizabeth. Essex died, however, and so regardless of the extent of their previous flirtations, Leicester and Lettice got married, quietly. As she was the Queen and it was her business to know everything, however quiet, Queen Elizabeth eventually found out, and was furious, famously calling Lady Lettice of Leicester a "She-Wolf" and banning her from court. She was also furious with the Earl of Leicester, but as he had been one of her favourites, she still permitted him in her presence from time to time, following the time-honoured pattern of women being more furious at the other woman than at the man.

Interestingly enough, Lady Lettice was mother to another one of Queen Elizabeth's favourites, the (2nd) Earl of Essex, whose history is too complicated to enumerate here, as that part of history takes place after my poem. Viewers at home may recall may recall Leicester as the man played by Joseph Fiennes in the first Cate Blanchett *Elizabeth*, and Essex as the man played by Hugh Dancy in the Helen Mirren mini-series *Elizabeth*. (By viewers at home I mean 'girls who watch too many historical dramas'.)

» **"To Nora", p.33**

I played Nora in Henrik Ibsen's *A Doll's House*. The play traces the relationship between Nora and her husband Torvald, one in which Nora has always had a playful and childish role. Secretly, however, she has been trying to budget household expenses, and engages in side-work in order to pay off a loan she took years ago from a disgraced lawyer to take care of Torvald when he was very ill. She always imagined that he would be grateful if she revealed her sacrifice to him, but as circumstances unravel and the many (and some of them, illegal) complications surrounding her loan are finally brought to light, Torvald's enraged response helps Nora realize that the foundation of their relationship is spurious. "I have existed merely to perform tricks for you, Torvald... I was your doll-wife," Nora explains, in the play's central metaphor, which I allude to lightly in "porcelain." Nora is onstage for most of the play, while the other characters rotate in (seemingly just to make her feel increasingly terrible), and it made for one of the more exhausting performances I've yet to experience. My three stanzas are meant to parallel the play's three acts.

» "My Mr. Paradise", p.34

I wrote this poem while performing in a production of *Five by Tenn*, a staging of five short plays by Tennessee Williams (there were, in fact, five plays and one scene in our production). I played, amongst others, the unnamed Girl in the beautiful piece *Mr. Paradise*, in which a young girl comes to seek an old poet whose volume of plays she found propping up the short leg of a tea-table in an antique shop in New Orleans. When I first read the play, I wept profusely (as is my wont), and chased down the opportunity to audition for the production. Though it would be easy to lie in order to fit this poem into this book, I did not write this poem *as* the Girl, but rather as myself, imagining if it were still possible for me to track down my own "father-poet," and to talk to him. The poem is wholly inspired by the *circumstance* of the play, however, and of Mr. Paradise's final vision of a time when the world will be ready to hear his poems again.

» "To Caroline", p.37

In Marina Carr's *By the Bog of Cats*, a contemporary retelling of *Medea* set in rural Ireland, Caroline is the parallel to Glauce, the woman for whom Jason leaves Medea in Euripides' play. Medea's Irish counterpart is named Hester, a woman of tinker (that is, Irish gypsy) heritage, and Jason's is named Carthage. Hester and Carthage's relationship began when Carthage was sixteen and Hester about ten years his senior, and now, roughly fifteen years later, Carthage is interested in taking a more respectable woman to wife. Caroline's father is a prosperous landowner, and there is certainly the insinuation in the play that Caroline is simply younger and wealthier, but not actually more beloved.

My experience doing Irish plays is always fed by what I know of Ireland, though I do not pretend to be any sort of expert. I have been there a half-dozen times with my father, who is a folklorist. He's lived with people in rural Ireland for extended periods of time, doing fieldwork (one of those people, Ellen Cutler, is my namesake). His most recent of five books about Ireland, *The Stars of Ballymenone*, came out earlier in the same year that I did *By the Bog of Cats*, and some things that I read in it came to mind when doing the play and writing these poems. The most prominent example in this poem is the fact that, in the community in which my father did fieldwork, poets were not also supposed to sing their own songs, as it would have been thought of as too arrogant. Conversely, by singing a song written by another local poet, a person strengthened the community.

» **"Caroline: The Unspoken", p.39**

See the previous note for some comments on plot and context. Carr presents a very lonely vision of this small, rural community, and loneliness dominated my consciousness while I was playing Caroline. There are only two people, as it seems, with whom she has any relationship—her father and her fiancé/husband—and both relationships are deeply troubled. Her father terrorizes her, and sexual abuse is strongly hinted, though not explicitly stated. One hopes her relationship with her husband Carthage will be some improvement, but he appears to be marrying her chiefly for her position and her land, and there is little intimacy, emotional or otherwise, in the relationship.

I find her plight particularly melancholic in the context of rural Irish culture, where the singing of songs, the playing of instruments, and the telling of stories or news were traditionally valued to keep the mind off the cold, hard life of farming and the long, dark nights. But Caroline, browbeaten and quiet, does not seem fit to offer chatter of any kind to save her from thinking about the hard facts of her own life. I find her situation sadly resonant, too, with the changes in contemporary rural Ireland. No one could argue about the merits of electricity, heating, and running water, but, as I understand it, it comes at a price of societal integration. Patterns of this phenomenon exist worldwide: we have email, so we talk to each other less. Dramaturgically speaking, Hester, the old lover, has an 'earth mother' quality to her, and a connection to tradition; Caroline, the new wife, is isolated, silent, and her modernity is like that of a family who never talks because they're always watching television.

The multiple references to ghosts in this poem reflect my impression of the prevalence of ghosts and ghost stories in traditional Irish culture, as well as their prominent position in Carr's play. I was terrified as a child by accounts, from one of my father's Irish friends, of a ghost hurling around the furniture in his room.

The capitalized "Room" in Section VIII refers to a custom, in some Irish houses, of having a room used almost exclusively to entertain visitors. The Room is kept clean, and only the other parts of the house, however small, are used for actual day-to-day living. It might be thought of as akin to a front parlour, or to a pristine living room in houses where the family only uses the den or family room. But I live in a one-bedroom New York apartment, so in fact, it's all speculation to me.

» **"The Director: To Galatea", p.45**

This is my one poem about directing, the first of only a few times I have had the experience. I wanted to direct in the hopes of understanding the whole process better, and becoming a better, more communicative, and collaborative actor. I think I did learn a great deal, and I think I was not a bad director, but being a director did not make me happy. I have learned that really what I like about theatre is playing with the other actors, so when the time came for performances, I felt like I was left out of the best part. This is also why I am uninterested in doing a one-person show. I would do so only as an alternative to having some other, non-theatre-related, job.

» **"World Premiere", p.46**

I was in the world premiere—that is, the first-ever production—of Janet Kenney's play *More Than What*. (I have been in several premieres, but the only other one mentioned in this volume is *The Yellow Leaf*, in the section titled "Mary.") My opening line's reference to "On First Looking into Chapman's Homer" struck me as an analogous situation; people who fancy they are Very Clever and point out that Keats didn't seem to know that Cortez didn't *discover* the Pacific seem to miss the point that Keats must obviously have known that he didn't *discover* Homer.

» **"Week Four Doldrums", p.50**

This was written on the occasion of some other actors in this production complaining that they were tired of doing the play. This can sometimes happen in longer runs, when the newness of the experience wears off, but closing is distant enough that the performances are not caught up in its momentum. I never say anything, but I have little patience with actors who complain about being bored. At the very least, I always think, "Or we could have a Real Job," because the fact remains that people basically pay us to play make-believe. Granted, I have never had a run of a play longer than a year, and I can't quite imagine what it would be to do a production on Broadway for several years running. Furthermore, the Week Four Doldrums also manifest themselves in my experience on some night when, no matter how hard I try, I can't quite believe in anything I'm doing. This will happen sometimes, regardless of my essential gratitude for simply being there. I often get the impression that non-actors think that actors are terrified of making a mistake, or forgetting their lines. In my experience, neither of these things make me cringe afterwards quite so much as simply feeling that a certain performance was Kind Of Off.

» **"Pegeen", p.51**

I did two productions of John Millington Synge's *Playboy of the Western World* in fairly quick succession, with only one other production sandwiched between. The first time, I played Sara Tansey, a fun but smaller role. What was very nice about playing Sara is that I basically alternated between hanging out backstage and going on stage and having a blast—there is little angst in the role. The only problem was that I've wanted to play Pegeen, the lead, since my very youth. I have a clear memory of my father once showing me a loy (a kind of heavy spade) when we were travelling in Ireland, explaining that it was the implement with which Christy Mahon hit his father over the head. (Clearly, this was a suggestion to read the play, not a suggestion from my father about tactics for fighting with farm tools.) So it was doubly a dream come true when I got cast as Pegeen four months after my first production had closed, and I threw myself precipitously into it. At another time in my life, this production would have occasioned a whole sheaf of poems, as I had an exceptionally wonderful director, a dream cast, and the performance was one of which I am most proud.

My lines "stuck just bringing in the petticoat / on his famous line about the shifts" refers to the fact that Sara brings a petticoat to disguise (and theoretically, to save) Christy at the end of Act III, and I took my cue to start running in from Christy's line, "It's Pegeen I'm seeking only, and what'd I care if you brought me a drift of chosen females, standing in their shifts itself, maybe, from this place to the Eastern World?" This line sparked the famous Playboy Riots, wherein a good portion of the audience at the opening performance in 1907 set to rioting at what they perceived as an affront to Irish womanhood. It was, in fact, merely the match to the powder keg, because the greater offence was Synge's portrayal of the Irish peasantry, who, at this time in Ireland's history, were typically depicted as noble and honest, in aid of Ireland's nationalist cause.

» **"To Emily", p.53**

I wrote this little poem while playing Emily Vernon in Arnold Bennett's *What the Public Wants*. The production was at the Mint Theatre, a jewel of a company, which specializes in reviving plays that have slipped from the public consciousness. Originally written in 1909, the play last received a production in the 1930s, and I found the process of figuring out an old play as if it were a new play—because we have no received information about it, as with, for example, *Pygmalion,* or *Playboy of the Western World*—a delight unparalleled. This is why I wrote that "only I (of those alive)" know Emily, under the assumption that the actress who played Emily in its last production is no longer with us. In rehearsal, I found that the actors playing other characters universally seemed to read Emily's character as a sort of female version of their own characters, when I found her to be far more complicated, and initially, at times, inscrutable. This, as well as that fantastical experience of watching an infinite parade of our own selves in parallel mirrors, fed my line (like a mirror to a mirror).

» **"For Mary (Present)", "For Mary (Departed)", pp.54-5**

I wrote these during and after a production of *Mary's Wedding,* a two-person play in which the other actor was my boyfriend of, at the time, two-and-a-half years. I expected it would be fun, but it was ten times more fun than I even thought it would be, with thanks to both himself and the director. The entire experience was as good as a day-dream. This beautiful play is challenging in the best sense: both actors are on stage the entire time, the scene moves backward and forward in time and space from Canada to the front in WWI, and I played not only the eponymous Mary but her love interest's sergeant in the army. I was doing some work on this collection while in this play, and consequently I labeled the poems "Present" and "Departed" as an echo of my Eliza poems, the earliest character poems to appear in this book.

» **"After the Death", p.56**

I have not consciously created gestures for my characters since I was in college. A character's gestures seem to evolve spontaneously during the rehearsal process out of the world of the play, her particular circumstances, and her needs. I simply find myself doing something which is unique to that character—certainly not my own, and usually not entirely like any other character's gesture, either, though some overlap exists. For example, "Queenfeet and sidethumb," in my poem "Pegeen," are names I gave to two of her gestures which were utterly surprising to me, and utterly, exclusively hers. What will happen, however, is that I will start unconsciously using these gestures myself, in my off-stage life. It makes me laugh if I do it while the play is still in performance, but after the show has closed, it always reminds me of coming across something once owned by a deceased loved one.

II. THOMASINA

My first production on an Equity stage was at the Publick Theatre in Boston, playing Thomasina in Tom Stoppard's *Arcadia*. (Actors' Equity is the union for professional actors and stage managers, and working in Equity theatres—that is, those that comply with the union's standards, and hire union actors—was an important step up for me as a young actor. I had done paid acting work beforehand, with non-union theatres, but working in union theatres provides a path for actors to join the union, and thus ensure standards of pay and working conditions for themselves. I am very thankful to Actors' Equity, because if anyone ever needed to be protected from being taken advantage of, it's actors. I am proud to have been a member since 2007.)

Being cast in this production remains one of the great blessings of my life, and I continue to feel indebted to Diego Arciniegas, the Artistic Director of the Publick and the director of *Arcadia*. Diego had only seen me play the *highly* comparable role of Malcolm in *Macbeth* (I am here being ironic) with the company ShakespeareNow, but nevertheless he took the chance with me. At twenty-two, I had fancied that I was probably too old to ever get to play Thomasina, and when I got the call about the role, I remember running, running and jumping and running, running and jumping and running, running and jumping down the long hallway of my Boston apartment. Not, apparently, too old.

I am not the only one who thought this production magical, as it won an Elliot Norton Award for Best Production. I, along with my co-star Lewis Wheeler in the role of Septimus, were also nominated for IRNE Awards for Best Actress and Actor, respectively.

The play, in and of itself, is phenomenally brilliant and brilliantly phenomenal. Thomasina's storyline takes place in 1809-12 on a country estate in Derbyshire called Sidley Park. At the play's start, Thomasina is thirteen years old, engaging in high-spirited discussions with her tutor, Septimus. Septimus's assignments occasionally frustrate her, but it seems to me that he is probably her best friend in the household. By the end of the play, she is seventeen, and her affection for him has grown from that of a young girl to that of a young lady. Thomasina, it turns out, is a mathematical genius, and quickly becomes exasperated with the classical geometry of her studies, longing instead to find the equations which govern nature. Throughout the play, she precociously comes to understand theories of contemporary math and physics which were not established in academia until well after her time, such as iterated algorithms, chaos theory, and the second law of thermodynamics. Stoppard weaves these theoretical concepts into the themes of the play.

» "To Thomasina", p.61

I wrote this poem the day in rehearsal when we were learning to waltz. Thomasina is desperate, in the final act, to learn how to waltz, and the play ends with Septimus teaching her to do so.

This production was at the Publick's outdoor space, on the banks of the Charles River, which meant we had to contend with passing rainstorms. As anyone who has worked in outdoors summer theatre knows, weather, along with passing boats, airplanes, and, on one memorable occasion, a medical helicopter, make performance a continued improvisation.

In my own, highly unmathematical nod to Thomasina's iterated algorithms, each stanza contains as many feet per line as lines per stanza.

Thomasina dies, as we are told in the play by the historians of the contemporary sections, in a fire on the night of her seventeenth birthday. This lies behind some of the imagery in this poem, also common themes of the Romantic poetry of the time, and, as I believe, part of the metaphorical resonances of the plays' events. Burning is also the best description I have for the palpable sensation of heat that sometimes grips my body in the middle of performance, a feeling that I am actually being consumed.

» **"Thomasina's Poem to Be Lost to the Sands of Time", p.63**

Lost documents are a key element in *Arcadia*. The "poet" referenced in the second line is Lord Byron, who is staying at the Coverly estate and figures importantly in various storylines, but does not appear onstage.

» **"To Thomasina, One Year Later", p.65**

A year after *Arcadia*, I was back working at the Publick again, doing *The Beard of Avon*. (You will probably guess this was a delightful experience for me, if you have perused my Geoffrey poems; it was.) But it wasn't our *Arcadia*; nothing ever will be, again. The previous summer, Thomasina-me had made the trees on the banks of the Charles into a part of Sidley Park (the name of the Coverly estate), and it was odd to see them *not* as Sidley Park. And it was odd to think that no doubt, in another production of *Arcadia*, running somewhere else precisely while I was in *The Beard of Avon*, someone else was looking at Sidley Park, and it looked nothing like I had seen. The piano metaphor in the first couple of lines draws from the piano playing that happens (off-stage) at a few different places in *Arcadia*. The endings of the first and last lines of each stanza are meant to echo the journey from the year before to the poem's present.

» **"To Thomasina, Six Years Later", p.66**

The fourth stanza refers to this exchange:

THOMASINA: When you stir your rice pudding, Septimus, the spoonful of jam spreads itself round making red trails like the picture of a meteor in my astronomical atlas. But if you need stir backward, the jam will not come together again. Indeed, the pudding does not notice and continues to turn pink just as before. Do you think this odd?

SEPTIMUS: No.

THOMASINA: Well, I do. You cannot stir things apart.

SEPTIMUS: No more you can, time must needs run backward, and since it will not, we must stir our way onward mixing as we go, disorder out of disorder into disorder until pink is complete, unchanging and unchangeable, and we are done with it for ever. This is known as free will or self-determination.

> » **"Candle for Thomasina, or, Theatrechurch's Failing", p.67**
>
> The line "I might put my grief to sleep" carries in it one of Thomasina's lines. When she is distraught at the thought of all the plays and knowledge lost when the library at Alexandria burned, she finishes, "How can we sleep for grief?" When I look now at Septimus's response, especially the line "We shed as we pick up, like travellers who must carry everything in their arms, and what we let fall will be picked up by those behind," it seems particularly resonant with the experience of being an actor.

III. RAINA

George Bernard Shaw's *Arms and the Man* was my last production in Boston before I moved to New York City. Since my first production there, out of college, had been *Pygmalion*, and since Spiro Veloudos, Artistic Director of the Lyric Stage and the director of *Arms and the Man* had been so kind as to hire me for my second production in Boston, *A Midsummer Night's Dream*, the experience had a balance to it, a coming-full-circle aspect, a thus-the-whirligig-of-time-brings-round-his-revenges aspect, as if my cherished time in Boston were a sandwich made of Shaw-Veloudos bread. It remains one of my favourite productions.

Raina (ra-EE-na) is a young Bulgarian woman, engaged to a man named Sergius, an officer in the Bulgarian war. The play opens during the Serbo-Bulgarian war, with the news that Sergius has taken the enemy in a cavalry charge. Both Sergius and Raina have heroic ideals, have read too much Byron, and talk to each other of achieving the Higher Love. Through-out the course of the play, however, both Sergius and Raina fall for someone else, Raina developing an affection for the thoroughly pragmatic Captain Bluntschli, a Swiss professional solider who happens to have signed up for the opposing (Serbian) army.

Blutschli's common sense cracks Raina's heroic aspirations, and though many people, Blutschli and Shaw among them, might call Raina's behaviour mere 'posturing,' I, as a person who loves Raina, think it's a manifestation of a desire to *be* better, grander, nobler, not merely to *act* that way. I think that she is inspired by poetic things because she does find an echo of her true self in them; her 'heroic attitude' is born out of a genuine impulse, that merely gets misplaced. Granted, I have also seen productions of this play that would beg to differ with my interpretation. But I think contemporary Americans view, or can view, *aspiration* in a different way than could the British at the end of the 19th century, where trying to work your way up in the world was an affront to the class system. The vast majority of us would be nothing and get nowhere if we didn't initially have some vision of our lives towards which we aspired, and I think Raina's transformation is about the discovery of the *true* nobility of the way Bluntschli leads his life, thus a completion, not an abandonment, of a course.

» **"Poem to Give to Sergius", p.71**

In Act I, Raina saves Captain Bluntschli by agreeing, after some argument, to hide him in her bedroom after he has clambered up to her balcony to escape a skirmish in the streets. She learns, however, that Blutschli was in the regiment that Sergius charged, and that his cavalry charge was only successful because Blutschli's regiment had been sent the wrong cartridges and couldn't fire their guns. Blunstchli describes a cavalry charge by saying, "It's like slinging a handful of peas against a windowpane: first one comes; then two or three behind him; then all the rest in a lump." Raina continually calls Bluntschli's attitude cowardly, but it is clear that she feels more affection for him than anything else by the end of the scene. I imagined that this would make it very difficult to write a poem for Sergius the following day. My/our initial taking-off point for the poem was Lord Byron's "The Destruction of Sennacherib."

» **"Raina's Poem: To a Photograph", p.72**

Raina and her mother bundle Captain Bluntschli off the following morning in one of Major Petkoff's (Raina's father's) old coats, and Raina slips a photograph of herself into one of its pockets, bearing the inscription: "Raina, to her Chocolate Cream Soldier—a souvenir." Bluntschli's return, months later, is facilitated by his wish to return the coat, and the hide-and-seek of the coat and the photograph create much comic intrigue in the play's final act. When Bluntschli reveals to Raina that he never found the photograph, and that he behaved (characteristically) unsentimentally with care of the coat, she is very offended and upset. I imagined, being sympathetic to her poetic imagination, that she must have endowed the photograph with a great deal of heart and significance, which is why the revelation hurts her so keenly. I wrote this poem in part to explore and make specific for myself exactly what the cost is to Raina. Also, I imagine this poem being the one she takes up after the previous one to Sergius fails, utilizing a simpler blank verse form.

» **"After the Last", p.74**

In this poem, I imagined Raina's life after the final moment of the play. I think I wrote it in an effort to keep her with me, to extend her life. But of course she has no life beyond the one the author gave her.

IV. MARY

Sometimes I am almost stopped midstep with the comprehension of how lucky I have been to have played so many gorgeous roles, like jewels in a necklace, like a laundry line of ballgowns, like a ladder of tremendous fortune. But I think the greatest of all these blessings was the chance I got to play Mary Shelley in the world premiere production of Charles Morey's *The Yellow Leaf*. The play centers on the famous-to-English-majors summer of 1816 at the Villa Diodati, close to Lake Geneva, when the great Romantics Percy Bysshe Shelley and George Gordon, Lord Byron, met. Cooped up due to the unseasonably cold and stormy weather afflicting Europe that summer, and inspired by a volume of ghost stories the group was reading, Byron proposed they write horror stories for each other. The fruit of this, in Mary's case, was her famous novel *Frankenstein*. Byron wrote a story that was picked up by his physician's assistant, John Polidori, and turned into the novel *The Vampyre*. As far as I know, Byron's/Polidori's was the first instance of a vampire in a work of written fiction (as opposed to oral tradition). So say thank you, *Twilight* fans.

Some autobiography is necessary to comprehend why this play was so special to me. Unlike many of my peers, I do not have any conservatory training in theatre. (This is part of why I feel so *lucky* to be making a living as an actor.) I entered college knowing I wanted to be an actor, but wanting more basic education than High School had afforded me. I graduated with a BA in English and Theatre, having taken only a few practical theatre classes, but having cobbled together a balanced, if uncredited, English/Theatre curriculum by additionally doing eleven plays in college and going to professional training programs during summer breaks. In my sophomore year, I had a fantastic professor, Andrew Stauffer, whose infectious enthusiasm taught me to love the English Romantics almost as much as I already loved Shakespeare. I focused my studies thereafter on 19th century English poetry, and in my senior year wrote a thesis on metapoetry through self-representation in Keats and Shelley. I think I read *Frankenstein* in three separate classes. When I graduated, I joked to a friend: "The only thing I'm fit to do now is play Mary Shelley in a play about Byron and the Shelleys." Dear reader, I kid you not.

Four years later, I had come off of a year-long tour with the American Shakespeare Center and was preparing to move to New York, shuttling back and forth from my mother's house in Philadelphia to go to auditions until I found a living situation. I did not have an agent, and was just going to general auditions held by the theatre union, Actors' Equity. I saw the notice for general auditions for Pioneer Theatre Company's season, which included a play listing Byron, Shelley, Mary Shelley, Claire Clairmont, and John Polidori as its characters. I think I physically jumped backwards from the callboard. As luck would have it—ultimately, it was good luck, though I didn't think so at the time!—I couldn't attend these general auditions. I emailed Charles Morey in despair, requesting to be seen for the particular auditions for the play, and explaining my personal love for and study of the English Romantics. I did not really think it would work, I just knew I had to do everything in my power to try.

In my experience, emailing the artistic director of a theatre does not usually get me an audition. However, Charles Morey is truly an extraordinarily kind human being, and took a chance on me. He'd never even met me, but he was moved by my plea as a devotee of the Romantics, and bolstered, as he would narrate the story to me later, by the fact that I correctly identified the allusion of the title. (See Mr. Morey's Foreword.) When I walked out of the audition, however, I was merely aware that I had not shamed Mr. Morey by bringing me in, and that, despite not knowing the director, artistic director, or casting director, and despite the fact that I wanted to do that play more than anything before in my life, I had not crumbled into nervousness. I thought in that moment, *This is the best day of my life.* The fact that I actually got the part made it even better, but it was already the best.

It is worth noting, in support of the '*Yellow Leaf* as Apotheosis of My Life' theory, that during that production I met both my agent, who represents

Charles Morey as a playwright and thus flew out to see the premiere, and my now-husband, who was rehearsing a production of *Romeo and Juliet* while I was in performance. Years later, I am still grateful to both of them every day, in very different ways.

» **"Epistles to Mary", p.80**

Percy called Mary his "child of light." I also refer to the fact that she wrote *Frankenstein* at the astonishing age of nineteen. In the second part of the poem, I refer to the fact that Percy Shelley loved doing experiments with electricity as a boy, occasionally involving his siblings. His rooms at University College, Oxford, were littered with all manners of scientific and electrical instruments. Scholars naturally speculate that this has something to do with Victor Frankenstein's use of electricity in animating his monster.

» **"Invocation: To Mary", p.81**

Percy in his boyhood was also obsessed with the desire to see a ghost, and would sleep in graveyards and crypts in the hopes of spotting one. The non-appearance of a ghost led to his self-identification as an atheist, though he was really to my mind more of an agnostic by modern definitions.

» **"For Mary", p.82**

I am in this poem cobbling together a few salient points, but a complete narrative and the greatest understanding can only come from perusing a full biography of Mary Shelley. I recommend *Mary Shelley: Her Life, Her Fiction, Her Monsters* by Anne Kostelanetz Mellor as my favourite, but also liked *Child of Light: Mary Shelley*, by Muriel Spark. The best are Mary's journals, but all the editions I found are fairly expensive. Fortunately, I had the University of Utah at my disposal at the time. An internet biography will also, as they say, beat a kick in the head. I'll lay out here a few biographical facts about Mary's life that may serve to illuminate the poem; others, I hope, will be obvious as I have implied them (for example, fact: Mary tended to get seasick).

Mary's father was the political philosopher, novelist and journalist, William Godwin. Different biographies of Mary paint slightly different pictures of the relationship between father and daughter, owing to the complex family situation—Mary's mother, Mary Wollestonecraft, feminist philosopher, died in childbirth, and William remarried a woman named Mary Jane Clairmont, with whom young Mary did not get along—but it is clear that Mary deeply revered and deeply loved her father.

Mary was Percy Shelley's second wife; at nineteen, he eloped with Harriet Westbrook. By the time Percy met Mary, three years later, he was largely estranged from his first wife and their daughter, and deeply unhappy with the marriage. He and Mary ran away for a trip on the continent, bringing along Mary's stepsister, Claire Clairmont. Mary became pregnant, likely during their trip, and experienced the first of her many heart-breaking miscarriages six months after returning to England. Despite being a radical and free-thinker, William Godwin had slightly different standards for his daughter, and did not support their unorthodox relationship. Mary, Percy and Claire lived in constant financial strain, moving, travelling or separating in order to escape creditors. The rift with her family was not healed until she and Percy were married, two years later—a possibility brought about when his first wife, Harriet, drowned herself in the Serpentine.

Nor was Harriet, before or after her death, the only woman preying on Mary's conscience. Percy and Claire were very close and spent a great deal of time together, often going out for whole days while Mary, frequently ill from childhood, was house-bound. Scholars wrestle in historical mud about whether or not Percy and Claire had a sexual relationship, but it is very clear that they were intimate, that Mary resented their intimacy, and that she continually sought arrangements in which she and Percy could have their own household, separate from Claire. I think I am not alone among women in feeling that if my partner were to be emotionally more intimate with another woman than he is with me, it would be just as bad as, and possibly worse, than sexual intimacy. The answer to the question, for me, about whether or not Percy and Claire slept together, is that it was bad enough, either way. My lines "I feel that fire poker come up every time / I hear he is with Claire" are about a moment in the play that Mary, seeking Percy, runs into Lord Byron, and he informs her that Percy is with Claire.

» **"Sonnet: The Painted Eye", p.85**

The reference in the title and in the final line of the poem is to Shelley's poem, "The Painted Veil." Its first half reads:

> *Lift not the painted veil which those who live*
> *Call Life: though unreal shapes be pictured there,*

And it but mimic all we would believe
With colours idly spread, —behind, lurk Fear
And Hope, twin Destinies; who ever weave
Their shadows, o'er the chasm, sightless and drear.

The second line is a reference to Shelley's *Epipsychidion,* quoted by Shelley in the play, and which constituted the cue before my speech:

I never was attached to that great sect
Whose doctrine is that each one should select
Out of the crowd a mistress or a friend,
And all the rest, though fair and wise, commend
To cold oblivion.

» **"No Adonais", p.86**

Shelley wrote the poem "Adonais" for Keats on the event of the latter's death. Though the production of *The Yellow Leaf* 'died young'—its run was only scheduled to be three weeks long—I was (as far as I'm aware) the only elegizing poet the show had. My feelings for my aptitude for this particular post are summed up in the title's negation.

» **"The Triumph of Death: For Mary", p.87**

In this poem I chronicle the deaths of Mary Wollestonecraft, her daughter Fanny, Shelley's first wife Harriet, the deaths of Mary's children (only one, Percy Florence, survived) one of her miscarriages, and finally Shelley's death. "The Triumph of Life" is a Shelley poem; in a great, sad irony, it was left unfinished at his death.

V. SHAKESPEARE
» **"Stratford", p.92**

I refer several times, in the first and fifth stanzas, to the lines written on Shakespeare's grave:

Good frend for Jesvs sake forbeare,
To digg the dvst encloased heare.
Bleste be ye man yt spares thes stones,
And cvrst be he yt moves my bones

"Would a mere player be buried in such state": It may not be so obvious to us now, when famous actors (chiefly those who work in television and film) appear on the covers of magazines, enticing people to look inside to view pictures of them doing things like taking their trash to the curb or sipping an iced latte, but in Shakespeare's day, actors were not judged as highly successful members of the population. My sense, which I think many actors living in New York or Los Angeles will sympathize with, is that actors were perhaps one class above cockroaches. Our scanty records of what happened to other players in Shakespeare's day indicate that they were more likely to die in penury than to be buried beneath the altar of a church. My suggestion: Shakespeare couldn't have gotten there if he'd only done things like play the ghost of Hamlet Senior.

The end of stanza seven can also be helped by some historical context. William Kempe is thought to have played many of Shakespeare's early comedic roles, often those of 'Clowns', that is, funny buffoons, often of lower class. Scholars speculate that Kempe may have played Dogberry in *Much Ado About Nothing*, Peter in *Romeo and Juliet*, Costard in *Love's Labours Lost*, Bottom in *A Midsummer Night's Dream*, and Lancelot Gobbo in *The Merchant of Venice*. Kempe left Shakespeare's company in 1600, and one can clearly see that a very different kind of comedian follows in Shakespeare's works: Robert Armin, who succeeded Kempe, is reputed to have played roles such as Touchstone in *As You Like It*, Feste in *Twelfth Night*, the Fool in *King Lear*, and Lavatch in *All's Well That Ends Well*. These are wise 'Fool' characters, rather than 'Clowns'. It's obvious that Shakespeare was writing *for* Kempe and then *for* Armin, which I suggest is good evidence of the fact that the author of these plays knew his actors, and was not a far-removed Lord writing in a tower. It may be that Kempe was ousted for pulling faces and 'speaking more than was set down for him' (*Hamlet*), but he was also famous in his day for his dancing and jigs. In 1600, following his departure from Shakespeare's company, he reportedly did a Morris dance from London all the way to Norwich, a distance of almost 100 miles. We know about this because he wrote an account of this exploit entitled *Kempe's Nine Days Wonder*. Thus my phrase: "after Kempe went dancing off."

» **"The Juliet Chronicles", p.95**

Section II, "Names": I imagine Juliet passing the time after Romeo leaves her balcony and the next time we see her, impatient for the Nurse's return. The Nurse describes her state to Romeo, "She had the prettiest sententious of it, you and rosemary." (II.iv.225) I'm alluding also to the famous "What's in a name?" (II.ii.45). The last stanza refers to the fact that the name 'Romeo' contains the words 'o me.'

Section V, "Ancient Damnation": This is a reference to Juliet's line, "Ancient damnation! O, most wicked fiend" (III.v.235), after the Nurse has counseled her to marry Paris. Also to the Nurse's lines in I.iii about Juliet being weaned from breastfeeding, "For I had then laid wormwood to my dug [...] When it did taste the wormwood on the nipple / Of my dug, and felt it bitter, pretty fool, / To see it tetchy and fall out with the dug!" (ll.26; 30-32)

Section VI: I imagine Juliet's dream while under the influence of the Friar's potion of seeming death. There are myriad references in the third stanza:

> For thou wilt lie upon the wings of night
> Whiter than new snow on a raven's back (III.ii.18-19)
>
> Dove-feathered raven! Wolfish-ravening lamb! (III.ii.76)
>
> and when he shall die,
> Take him and cut him out in little stars (III.ii.21-22)
>
> And shrieks like mandrakes torn out of the earth (IV.iii.47)
>
> Or walk in thievish ways; or bid me lurk
> Where serpents are; chain me with roaring bears (IV.i.79-80)
>
> Saints do not move, but grant for prayer's sake (I.v.107)
>
> That which we call a rose
> By any other word would smell as sweet (II.ii.45-46)

The following stanza refers to "Such a wagonner / As Phaeton would whip you to the west, / And bring in cloudy night immediately" (III.ii.2-4).

When Juliet wakes in the tomb, her first line is "I do remember well where I should be." I am considering waking to find Romeo dead as an event that continually happens to Juliet the character—it happens night after night, production after production, century after century, a treatment of the idea of a character found, for example, in Pirandello's *Six Characters in Search of an Author*, and Tom Stoppard's *Rosencrantz and Guildenstern Are Dead*, and in Ryan Landry's *M*, a production I was part of seven years after writing this poem. The line "What lamb, what lady, why bride," is from Act IV, scene v, where the Nurse discovers Juliet apparently dead from the Friar's potion.

» "The Five Acts of Lady M", p.102

The 'o's of the first three stanzas becoming 'oh, oh, oh' in the fourth is a reference to the line, as written in the edition I was working with, "All the perfumes of Arabia could not sweeten this little hand. Oh, oh, oh!" The final stanza, signifying the fifth act of the play, refers to Macbeth's famous speech upon receiving word of her death, "She should have died hereafter. / There would have been time for such a word. / Tomorrow and tomorrow and tomorrow / Creeps in this petty pace… " Because her last scene is the first scene of Act V, the character in fact literally becomes the reference to herself in this speech.

» "The Diana Chronicles", p.103

Diana is a character in what may be my favourite of Shakespeare's lesser-known works, *All's Well That Ends Well*. I was exceedingly fond of this play long before I had done a single production of it.

Section I: "Every night he comes / With musics of all sorts" (III.vi.39-40) is a line of the Widow's (Diana's mother), describing Bertram coming to woo Diana by bringing musicians to her window. I imagine in this what it is like for Diana, hearing the serenade, but knowing that she cannot do anything about it, since Bertram is married to Helena. I reference also the Elizabethan belief in "the music of the spheres," that the Earth and the heavens are in fixed concentric circles which create a celestial harmony as they revolve and align.

Section II: In the scene in which they meet (IV.ii), Bertram tells Diana, "If the quick fire of youth light not your mind / You are no maiden, but a monument." (ll.5-6).

Sections III and IV: These are the imagined sentiments of Diana before and after the bed trick, respectively. Afterwards she follows Helena to France (V) to set her plea before the King of France (VI).

» "Kill the Boys", p.106

The title refers to Fluellen's line "Kill the boys and the luggage!" (IV. vii.1), after the French soldiers, enraged by their imminent loss of the battle, have gone through the English camp and killed the young unarmed boys who were guarding the "luggage" of the English soldiers' personal items. In this production of *Henry V*, at the wonderful American Shakespeare Center where they try to remain true to 'original staging practices,' Fluellen brought me out on stage on a bloodied sheet, with a bloody scarf binding my neck—a solution a little more low-tech than using contemporary stage blood, but which I think was chiefly necessitated by my quick change into Princess Katherine after a scene as the dead boy.

Other references in this poem are to Macbeth's famous "Tomorrow and tomorrow" after learning Lady Macbeth has died: "To the last syllable of recorded time" (V.v.21); to Lear's equally-famous lines lamenting Cordelia, "Thou'lt come no more, / Never, never, never, never, never!" (V.iii.307-08); and to Exeter's lines "And all my mother came into mine eyes / And gave me up to tears" (IV.vi.31-32), describing the death of the Duke of York, in the previous scene of *Henry V* (so I remember listening to our Exeter recite those lines as I was trying not to cry).

Henry V has been one of my favourite plays, ever since Kenneth Branagh's screen version was my first exposure to Shakespeare at the age of seven (I loved it so much, I made my parents take me back to see it five times—thus, the nerd I am). I found both the Boy and Princess Katherine to be exceptionally joyful characters to play, and I was very sad to bid them adieu.

» **"Portia", p.107**

Ours was a year-long contract at the American Shakespeare Center (our other plays were the previously mentioned *Henry V* and *Taming of the Shrew*, as well as *A Christmas Carol* at the appropriate seasonal time), so I spent a very long time with Portia, beginning with the moment I learned I would be playing her and began working on my script.

Portia gets a bad rap. I am of the opinion that she discovers, just as I discovered that year, that what you do and how you feel about who you are, at any given moment, have far more to do with your environment and your circumstances than an intrinsic character of the self.

» **"Wound", p.109**

In a biographical sidenote that has the last laugh, three of the scratches I acquired in the fashion described are still faintly visible as scars.

» "Lady Percy and I Attend a Dress Rehearsal", p.110

This poem and the previous are about a production of *Henry IV, Part One* in which I played Lady Kate Percy, wife to Hotspur. I have always, always loved Lady Percy. I had long held her out as an example of one of those roles I would much rather play than others with many more lines (Lady Percy only appears in two scenes in Part One, and only one in Part Two, a fact I reference in this poem). I wrote a paper about her in college, had done her monologue in Part Two for years, played her as a student at Shakespeare & Company... consequently, when I finally did the full production, I already felt very close to her. The rehearsal process, with a very eloquent and patient director, only strengthened this feeling. I became saddened when I watched, during a dress rehearsal, the final battle in which Prince Hal kills Hotspur. This led me also to contemplate the life of Lady Percy as a character, suffering a continual inevitable loss, much the same way as I thought about Juliet always waking, in the infinite suspended present moment of all fiction, to find Romeo dead in "The Juliet Chronicles."

The name of Henry Percy's wife was in historical fact Elizabeth, but Shakespeare changed it to Kate. Perhaps he thought it prudent to not give the Queen's name to someone on the side of rebellion? It is interesting that he changed her name to be the same as Henry V's wife, so in fact, it is two Harrys, eventually wedded to two Kates, battling each other in this play—which also meant I played two Kates, married to two Harrys, within a year.

In the third stanza I reference Hotspur's lines, "That roan shall be my throne!" (II.iii.73) and "Oh, I could prophesy" (V.iv.83). Hotspur's line about his horse in the scene with Lady Percy always struck me as a terrifying signal for his wife that his machinations include designs on the throne—whether that means crowning Mortimer, or an unconscious desire to be king himself. Certainly Shakespeare has many characters make the suggestion, early in the play, that Hotspur would seem to make a better King than Hal. The latter line, part of Hotspur's death speech, is a change from when Hotspur quite hilariously mocks Glendower for saying that he has prophetic powers in Act III, scene 1. Lines 148-164 in particular make me laugh aloud even when I read them.

The final line of the poem refers to Hotspur's line, "The King hath many marching in his coats" (V.iii.26), describing a battlefield ploy of King Henry IV's to dress many other Lords up as if they were the King—in essence, to create decoy Kings. The Douglas, for example, bags himself Sir Walter Blunt, who is dressed up like the King and claims to be him when asked. The idea has interesting implications for actors.

» **"Helena", p.112**

After at least a decade of desperately wanting to play Helena in *All's Well That Ends Well* (sorry, Diana), the lovely folks at the Shakespeare Theatre of New Jersey let me. I have loved Helena, for her intelligence, for her unique spirituality, and for her absolutely breathtaking language, and I have always empathized with her deeply as I myself have a very long history of being in love with, well, jerks. Rosalind in *As You Like It* remains my favourite, but I have always fancied that I am more like Helena than I am any other Shakespeare heroine. This very idea became a problem for me during the rehearsal of the production, because for years and years, in visiting and revisiting the play, I had braided my experience of being in love with inconsiderate men into my love of the text, and I had a difficult time, in fact, separating the character from myself. This was a great disservice to her, because she is a much better person than I am. I am indebted to the brilliant director of this show for being so patient and so persistent with me, as this proved one of the larger challenges of my life thus far, but I was proud of the work he helped me to attain. I lament that this, like the production of *Playboy of the Western World* that came right before it, yielded only this one very small poem, an unfitting tribute in both cases to playing, finally, roles I'd long dreamed about. But the truth is, Helena needs no poems of mine; she is better than that.

I use some of Helena's language in this poem. The fourth stanza refers to the lines about Bertram "'Twere all one / That I should love a bright particular star / And think to wed it, he is so above me" (I.i.86-88) and those about her father, "that his good receipt / Shall for my legacy be sanctified / By the luckiest stars in heaven" (I.iii.575-577). I suggest that I will be sanctified by becoming Helena, the same way her father's memory will be sanctified through the heaven-guided success of her task. The final stanza borrows "dull" from "only doth backward pull / Our slow designs when we ourselves are dull" (I.i.220-221), and "merit" from "who ever strove / To show her merit that did miss her love?" (I.i.228-229). These may seem small points, as I may un- or half-consciously borrow words from my character, in this poem and others; however, I quite specifically included these as references to these two lines, which I felt were also apt summaries of the attempt that I myself, as the actor, was making.

VI. ACTORS

This section contains poems written to, or largely about, other actors, outside the world of the play. Given my historical likelihood of dating or falling in love with actors, I have a *rather large* number of poems which have been written to actors, but I include here only those poems that also have reference or connection to the theatre.

» **"Romeo", p.119**

The last line of the fifth stanza is a truncated line of Juliet's: "I must hear from thee every day in the hour, / For in a minute there are many days. / O, by this count I shall be much in years / Ere I again behold my Romeo" (III.v.44-47). This line has always been one of my favourites, and has always made me sad.

» **"Love Triangle", p.121**

The three points of the triangle are myself, my character, and the other actor; the character is the 'you' addressed. The final lines refer to Hercules' eleventh labor, the command to steal the golden immortality-giving apples of the Garden of Hesperides. Hercules tricks Atlas into getting the apples for him by taking on, for a time, the burden of the sky. I assume the Garden of Eden apple reference in the second stanza will be familiar to more readers. By means of these allusions, science, religion, and myth are thus each invoked, forming another triangle, of central (and ultimately more lasting) significance to my own pattern of thought.

» **"This Life Denies Us", p.124**

The second stanza makes reference to Horace Walpole's epigram, "This world is a comedy to those that think, a tragedy to those that feel." The Shakespeare plays I reference, following, are *Antony and Cleopatra, Romeo and Juliet* and *Henry IV, Part 1*. The final two lines refer to the Scottish play, when Macbeth receives the witches' prophecy about whether or not Banquo's descendants will rule Scotland. He sees a procession of eight kings, the last, resembling Banquo, holding a mirror, in which Macbeth sees many more kings.

The third line of the final stanza refers to Yeats' "Lapis Lazuli":

Yet they, should the last scene be there,

The great stage curtain about to drop,

If worthy their prominent part in the play,

Do not break up their lines to weep.

They know that Hamlet and Lear are gay;

Gaiety transfiguring all that dread.

» **"After the War", p.125**

This poem was written about working for the first time with my sweet boyfriend of, at the time, two-and-a-half years (he since has become my husband). We met at a theatre, though we were working on different shows. The title and the final line refer, obnoxiously, to one of my own poems, the problem set up in the second part of the poem "The Actress," which can be found in the following section.

» **"Unacting", p.126**

I often find myself in other circumstances returning, as to a prayer, to the final stanza of this poem.

VII. AN ACTOR'S LIFE

» **"Thanks-giving in the Theatrechurch", p.130**

The "ancient wheel" I address in the second stanza is a reference to the wheel of fortune of the medieval, rather than game show, era, a concept often alluded to in Shakespeare.

» **"Theatre Sickness", p.132**

The third line refers to the Shakespeare's Sonnet 57, "Being your slave, what should I do but tend / Upon the hours and times of your desires?" The sonnet was brought to mind by talking with a fellow actor who used the word 'slave' in explaining his relationship to theatre. This is probably the earliest poem of mine to appear in this volume, but many years later, upon revisiting Shakespeare's sonnet, I am struck that theatre is not much unlike the master it describes, and many an actor would probably sympathize with such a reading of that sonnet, if perhaps an ironic one.

» **"Song of the Young Poet", p.134**

"To His Heart, Bidding it Have No Fear," is a Yeats poem, which, for its admirable brevity, and for the fact that I reference the majority of its lines, may be included in its entirety here:

> Be you still, be you still, trembling heart;
> Remember the wisdom out of the old days:
> Him who trembles before the flame and the flood,
> And the winds that blow through the starry ways,
> Let the starry winds and the flame and the flood
> Cover over and hide, for he has no part
> With the lonely, majestical multitude.

The second and third lines of the third stanza refer to one of my life-long favourites, Henry's "ceremony" speech from *Henry V*: "And what art thou, thou idol ceremony?" (IV.i.221).

» **"Tomorrow and Tomorrow and", p.137**

This speech of Macbeth's is one of my favourite pieces of English (I'm hardly alone in this opinion), and wins the unprestigious prize for being most often referred to in this volume (I'm hardly alone in referring to it—my reverence to Faulkner, Vonnegut). I think it was called to my mind in writing this by using the word "significance" in the first line; *cf.* "full of sound and fury / signifying nothing."

The metaphors of the "poor player" and the "brief candle" are carried throughout the stanza.

» **"The Year of Roving Approaches", p.138**

The poem is a contemplation of my (at the time) upcoming year-long touring contract. The full poem includes one section per month.

» **"Birthday", p.145**

Fanny Brawne was John Keats' love; problems of money and station precluded an official engagement, and Keats died at 25 without an engagement ever coming to pass, much less a marriage.

The penultimate stanza refers to Yeats' poem "The Choice," probably the English language quatrain I quote most frequently:

The intellect of man is forced to choose
perfection of the life, or of the work,
And if it take the second must refuse
A heavenly mansion, raging in the dark.

» **"The Actress", p.147**

In the fifth stanza, the question "What country, friends, is this?" is a line of Viola's from *Twelfth Night* (I.ii.1).

» **"To Actors Shooting a Commercial", p.149**

In one very lucky month, I was cast in three commercials—experiences and paychecks for which I'm thankful. However, being driven out to mansions on Long Island or in New Jersey for three consecutive weeks did cause me to think about the discrepancy between my actual life and the lives of the wives and mothers that I was portraying in the commercials. In a circumstance that adds another layer to these differences, I had also been working on memorizing many lines for a Shakespeare play at the same time, with the result that when I wrote the poem I more-or-less vomited it out in blank verse.

» **"Life's a Colander", p.150**

I wrote this poem shortly after I first moved to New York, over a year and a half before I played Helena at the Shakespeare Theatre of New Jersey, and it stands as one example of my long relationship with Helena, as alluded to in my poem named after her. It also stands as an example of "a blend of life and art," as expressed in my poem "After the War," the addressee of that poem and this being the same, sweet man.

Additionally, "Sometimes affection hits us like a pan" may be the most pleasing line of blank verse I have written yet.

ABOUT THE AUTHOR

A professional actor, Ellen Adair has
performed in dozens of professional
theatrical productions off-Broadway,
regionally, and touring the country,
as well as numerous television shows,
independent films and webseries.
She serves as Artistic Director of the
Happy Few Theatre Company. She lives
in Queens with her husband and their
dog, Mabel. Clips, reviews, and other
information about her life on stage and
screen can be found at *ellenadair.com*.

www.ingramcontent.com/pod-product-compliance
Lightning Source LLC
Chambersburg PA
CBHW022008090426
42741CB00007B/935